Software Quality Assurance

Tom Manns and
Michael Coleman

School of Information Science
Portsmouth Polytechnic

M
MACMILLAN
EDUCATION

First published 1988

Published by
MACMILLAN EDUCATION LTD
Houndmills, Basingstoke, Hampshire RG21 2XS
and London
Companies and representatives
throughout the world

Photoset by Ponting–Green Publishing Services, London
in association with Parker Typesetting Service, Leicester

Printed in Hong Kong

British Library Cataloguing in Publication Data
Manns, Thomas
  Software quality assurance.—(Macmillan computer science series).
  1. Computer systems. Software. Quality control
  I. Title   II. Coleman, Michael, *1946, May 12*
  005'.14
  ISBN 0-333-45990-3
  ISBN 0-333-45991-1 Pbk

Contents

To John and Grace Coleman

Abbreviations

ANSI – American National Standards Institute
APSE – Ada Programming Support Environment
ASQC – American Society for Quality Control
BSI – British Standards Institution
CADES – Computer Aided Development and Evaluation System
CAIS – Common APSE Interface Set
CORE – Controlled Requirement Expression
DOD – US Department of Defense
DTI – Department of Trade and Industry
EEA – Electronic Engineering Association
ESPRIT – European Strategic Program for R and D in Information Technology
IEEE – Institute of Electrical and Electronics Engineers
IPSE – Integrated Project Support Environment
MAPSE – Minimal Ada Programming Support Environment
PCTE – Portable Common Tool Environment
PERT – Project Evaluation and Review Technique
SREM – Software Requirements Engineering Methodology

Preface

Software is a complex product. It has been described in many standards as 'all instructions and data which are input to a computer to cause it to function in any mode; it includes operating systems, supervisory systems, compilers and test routines as well as application programs'. It also includes 'the documents used to define and describe the program (including flow charts, network diagrams and program listings)' as well as 'specifications, test plans, test data, test results and user instructions'.

Quality assurance can be described as

'a planned and systematic pattern of all actions necessary to provide adequate confidence that the item or project conforms to established technical requirements'.

It should be intuitively obvious from these definitions that software quality assurance is difficult, and likely to remain so. Expected developments in software engineering will not necessarily make the task any easier. It seems likely that difficulties in one area will be reduced and difficulties in other areas created or increased. For instance, a major problem in the near future will be the validation of complex, productivity-enhancing software development tools which have the potential to improve software quality significantly. In general, the greater our ability objectively to measure and control aspects of software and its development process, the more likely we are to be able to produce software of the required quality. Unfortunately, our ability in these areas is currently fairly limited and not increasing very rapidly.

This book addresses the unique problems associated with the software development process which a software quality assurance programme has to tackle. In doing so, it clearly aims to be of benefit to those involved in the business of assuring software quality. But quality cannot be added; it has to be built in. Since software quality, therefore, is ultimately in the hands of the developer, it is hoped that this book will also be read with profit by all involved in, or studying, the software development process.

Very broadly, the text is in two parts, both of which follow the conventional life cycle model. Chapters 1–5 deal with what could be termed the 'externals' of software quality assurance: planning, managing and reviewing. Chapters 6–9 focus on the 'internals': building quality into software during its development. Chapter 8 contains some material previously published by Chartwell-Bratt (*Software Engineering for Students*, M J Coleman and S J Pratt, 1986) to whom thanks are due.

The authors would also like to acknowledge the assistance they have received: from Malcolm Stewart of Macmillan Education, from the reviewers and from the many members of staff of the Ministry of Defence Directorate General of Defence Quality Assurance with whom they have discussed the topic.

T S Manns, M J Coleman
Portsmouth 1988

1 Introduction

1.1 Problems of defining software quality

The word quality is used in everyday speech to describe the degree of excellence of a product or service. Translating that apparently simple concept into a form in which it can be satisfactorily embodied into a legally enforceable contract between customer and supplier for software is surprisingly difficult.

The problem of defining quality is a general one: it is not peculiar to software. A good analysis of the problem is given by Garvin (1984), who argues that there are a number of different approaches to defining quality arising from different disciplines, all of which may be relevant.

Garvin's five approaches to defining quality are as follows:

Transcendent approach
In this approach, which originates from philosophy, the quality of a piece of software is viewed as its innate excellence. Quality is an unanalysable property.

Product-based approach
The quality of a piece of software is related to the presence of some attributes or characteristics.It implies that the quality of software is objectively measurable and that software products could be ranked in order of quality. Given the state of the art in software engineering, it may well be the case that not all the relevant attributes have been identified and that it is not known how to measure objectively some of the attributes that have been identified. So far as the measurement of the attributes is concerned, it seems likely that some attributes will either be present or not, for example portability, whereas others will be present to a greater or a lesser extent, for example complexity.

If one assumes that the provision of these attributes requires the use of resources, then there may be a positive relationship between the cost of software and its quality.

User-based approach
The quality of a software product is related to its fitness for use in a particular application. In this approach the quality is positively related to (or equated with) the software user's satisfaction with the software product in any given application.

Value-based approach
This appears to combine quality, which is a measure of excellence, with value, which is a measure of worth, by defining a quality product as one which provides performance at an acceptable price or conformance at an acceptable cost.

Manufacturing approach
Traditionally this approach has been concerned with engineering and manufacturing practice and is summarised in the expression 'make it right first time'. Quality is equated with conformance to stated requirements. For instance, the design of the software system would have been checked to ensure that if implemented it would meet the stated requirements; any subsequent deviation from a formally approved design would be seen as a reduction in quality. A deviation from the design would appear as a problem later in the software system's life cycle. This approach, by emphasising the prevention of defects, can be seen as a part of a policy to minimise the costs of production. The cost of rectifying errors discovered later in the software life cycle can be very high. It also leads to the reliability engineering of software, that is, the analysis of the design to identify possible problem areas, perhaps by the use of control and data flow complexity measures and the consideration of alternative designs.

Garvin suggests that there are a number of different dimensions of quality which may be of importance when considering the quality of a software product. These are:

Performance and features
The distinction between these two seems a little strained, but performance relates to the primary operating characteristics of the software and features refer to the secondary characteristics that supplement the software's basic functions.
Both of these dimensions are measurable but it does not follow that the user perceives differences between different vendors' software as significant in quality terms.

Reliability
There is the probability of a software product failing within a specified

period of time. This is a very difficult concept to define for software since it does not physically deteriorate.

Conformance

This aspect is concerned with the extent to which the output of each phase of the software development process meets the specification for that phase. The implications for the software developer are that the software should be 'tested' at each phase of its development, not only after coding has started. This dimension is of significance, both before and after acceptance of the software by the customer. Deviations may become apparent only after the software system has gone into service.

Durability

This is intended to be a measure of the length of time that the software can be used before replacement. There are many reasons for wishing to replace software. Some are related to the cost of changing it to meet new circumstances. For instance, it may be necessary to port it to new hardware to continue using it and replacement may seem preferable, or the complexity of the software may have increased so much as a result of changes to fix bugs or incorporate new features that further maintenance is felt to be more costly than purchasing a new product.

Serviceability

This aspect encompasses such things as the responsibility for rectifying defects, the length of time that this takes and the ease with which the supplier of the software accepts responsibility.

Aesthetics

Software can be beautiful, but what counts as beauty at any moment in time and how it is perceived is a matter for the individual.

Perceived quality

The individual whose opinion is sought about the quality of the software may not have full information about it and his or her opinion of its quality may be biased by, amongst other things, its price or the reputation of its supplier.

Even if one does not fully accept Garvin's analysis it seems clear that quality is not easily defined, except arbitrarily, and also that there are a number of dimensions to it. For software, probably the most common definition of quality is user-based, closely followed by the manufacturing-based definition.

The now standard definition of quality is:

'the totality of features and characteristics of a product or service that bear on its ability to satisfy a given need' (BSI 1979),

or alternatively,

'the degree to which the attributes of the software enable it to perform its specified end item use' (DOD 1985).

The concept of grade is useful in other areas of discussion about product quality and ought to be applicable to software. One could distinguish different conceptions of software which would satisfy a given need based upon such things as performance, diversity of functions provided, etc. Each of the concepts could be thought of as defining a different grade of the software, and software within these grades could be of high or low quality.

A quality profile model has been proposed by Kaposi and Kitchenham (1987) as a way of structuring the analysis of the quality of a piece of software (see Figure 1.1). The quality profile of the software is specific to an individual but has the advantage of separating quantifiable and non-quantifiable factors. Although more work remains to be done on the model, it provides a good basis for an explanation of why different people can simultaneously hold different views about the quality of the same piece of software.

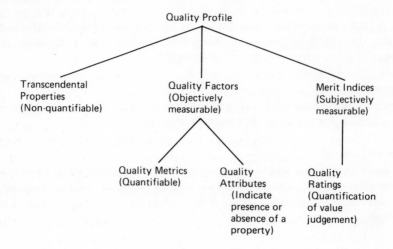

Figure 1.1

1.2 An overview of software quality assurance

The definition of software quality assurance is arbitrary, as one might expect, given the lack of a definition of quality encompassing all the associations of the word. The generally accepted definition is that given by ANSI/IEEE (1981):

'A planned and systematic pattern of all actions necessary to provide adequate confidence that the software conforms to established technical requirements.'

The form

'A planned and systematic pattern of all actions necessary to provide adequate confidence that the software conforms to a given specification'

is also widely used, particularly by the procuring agencies.

It should be clear from the definitions that the problems associated with the meaning of the word 'quality' have been avoided by assuming that it has been defined in terms of technical requirements or in the given specification. The clear statement of quality requirements in the requirements specification is a major step towards the production of good-quality software.

The assurance that the software is of good quality is to be provided by the application of a plan covering all activities undertaken during the software life cycle. These activities relate to the use of appropriate software construction techniques, as well as verification and validation activities.

Obviously, therefore, software quality assurance is very dependent upon management attitudes and skills. Software developers must apply three groups of disciplines, sometimes referred to as the discipline triangle, to produce software successfully. These three groups contain management, software development and product assurance disciplines. The development disciplines involve such things as analysis, design, testing, etc. The product assurance disciplines include quality assurance, test and evaluation, and configuration management. The management disciplines include both project and general management.

It is easy to identify the major categories of determinants of the quality of a product and from this one ought to be able to say something about how that quality can be assured and controlled. In the case of software these determinants are the specification, and the capital and labour resources of the developer.

The customer's needs must be fully and correctly translated into a system specification. This will be based upon the purpose for which the product must be fit and is thus central to the concept of quality.

Many facets of the labour resource are significant – numbers, skills, experience and training, for example. There is accumulating evidence that the use of automated techniques makes for better quality software and this requires capital investment.

The differences between software and hardware are well known and imply that the equivalent of the manufacturing stage for hardware is the design stage of the software. A moment's reflection about the nature of software defects will show that all defects must be designed into the software.

It is probably true to say that moving from the requirements specification to a good design is the most critical step in software development. There are three ways to convince oneself that a piece of software is free from defects:

- exhaustive testing
- a correct mathematical proof of correctness
- assurance that the output from each phase of the development process which will be a different representation of the software is functionally equivalent to its predecessor

In practice, a limited attempt is made at the third of these, unless formal methods are used. It is harder to show that the design is functionally equivalent to the specification than it is to show that the output of any other phase is functionally equivalent to its predecessor.

Software quality assurance accordingly lays considerable stress on getting the design right prior to coding, although the increasing use of prototyping in systems development is reducing the differences between the production stages of hardware and software.

There is obviously a stage in the production of software during which the software is repeatedly produced for transmission to customers, and it could be argued that this is the equivalent of the manufacturing stage in the production of hardware. We would not agree with this view. With good configuration management techniques this replication is a straightforward process and should pose few quality assurance problems.

The processes used to design, build and test the software are related to the facilities available to the developer and hence to the company's financial resources. Many potentially very costly tools, such as analysts' workbenches and IPSEs (Integrated Project Support Environment), seem likely to reduce the cost of producing good-quality software as they are developed and come into general use. These tools must of course be shown to work satisfactorily before they can be approved for use in software development. This is not likely to be easy or cheap if the problems involved in compiler validation are any indication of the effort required.

The attitude that problems can be sorted out at the end of the development process is changing, but changes in managerial attitudes are still needed. A much greater desire to produce a high-quality product resulting in a willingness to commit resources to do this, is required. Software developers must plan and implement software development projects with the objective of building in quality. It seems to be generally agreed that this involves activities in three distinct areas:

1. Establishment and maintenance of a requirements specification
This should be used as the basis for acceptance tests.

2. Establishment and implementation of a process for developing the software
The activities and functions involved in this process would usually be described in the developer's codes of practice (standards). In many cases these will be based upon internationally agreed standards, for example the various ANSI/IEEE standards. This area of activity includes project planning and, as part of this, it is important to establish a schedule of the major milestones early in a software development project.

3. Establishment and maintenance of an evaluation process
This will cover the software, its associated documentation and the software development process itself. This third area of activity, which is carried out at various points during the development of the software, is known as quality control.

In the UK, the British Standards Institution (BSI) has laid down standards which provide a general description of a process for the production of high-quality products. This can be found in BSI (1987). The individual software developer has to translate this general description into a production process. This involves the production of standards defining what must be done to complete a task successfully and also how the work should be done. These standards are often based upon other internationally agreed standards for such things as requirements specifications, configuration management plans, etc. Developers can apply to the BSI to be assessed and, if they have met the standards laid down, they will be registered as having met the requirements of the national standard. This provides some assurance that the the software that they produce will be satisfactory. The number of software developers who have been registered under this scheme is still very small, but it is to be hoped that more will come forward.

1.3 Software characteristics tree

A product-based approach to the quality of any particular class of software product results in the posing of questions such as 'what attributes or characteristics are relevant?' and 'how can they be measured?'

A list of attributes might include:

- efficiency
- reliability
- usability
- extendability
- portability
- testability
- understandability
- re-usability
- maintainability
- interoperability
- integrity
- survivability

An interesting derivation of some of these attributes from high-level user-oriented objectives (thus reflecting the user-based approach) can be found in Boehm *et al.* (1980). It is argued that the utility of a software product to the user is related to, *inter alia*, the effort required to use it as it is, the ease with which it can be maintained and whether or not it can be used on different machines.

This relationship can be shown in a tree structure (see Figure 1.2).

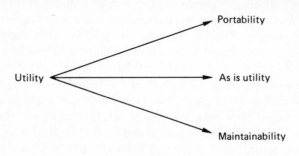

Figure 1.2

There is a logical implication denoted by the arrows. The tree can be read (using a non-exclusive *or*) as stating that if a piece of software has utility then either it is useful as it is, or it is portable to another machine, or it is maintainable.

The high-level attributes can themselves be shown to depend on other characteristics. For instance, if a piece of software is to be maintainable it must be understandable, testable and modifable. Given the state of the art in software engineering, growing the tree in this way until the characteristics at its leaves are objectively measurable may not yet be possible but it is a necessary goal if software quality assurance is to develop.

The approach has been called the quality factor, quality criteria, quality metric model. In abstract terms the tree structure can be decomposed as in Figure 1.3.

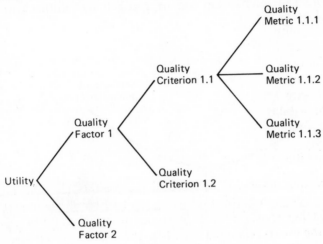

Figure 1.3

The list of attributes given earlier would be considered as quality factors in this approach.

The model can be applied to a specific product without too many conceptual problems, but there are many difficulties that arise if one tries to generalise it to apply to all software products in the abstract. Compare the list of quality factors that you would consider appropriate for the software embedded in a heat-seeking missile guidance system with that which you would consider appropriate for a microcomputer-based payroll system aimed at a large market. It is highly unlikely that the intersection set will contain all the factors, and it is not clear what can sensibly be done about this problem.

For any given class of software products it is unlikely that you could produce a set of mutually exclusive quality factors without a lot of effort. It is not obvious how one can sensibly show the conflicts (if they exist) between the quality factors for that class of software product. Maintainability is often alleged to conflict with speed of execution or minimisation of storage utilisation.

Researchers are attempting to derive a general constructive quality model, and Kitchenham (1987) describes the current position in a readable way.

1.4 Aspects of the relationship between software quality and cost

The conventional wisdom is that increasing quality reduces total costs up to some point. The relationship can be graphed by plotting cost against quality level (Figure 1.4).

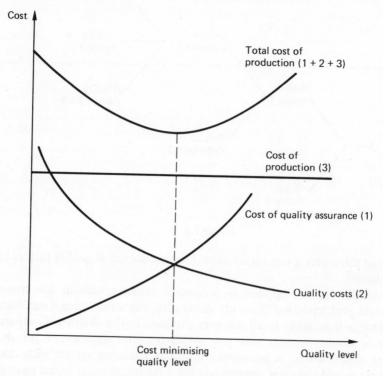

Figure 1.4 Relationship between quality and cost

Quality costs refer to the cost of correction of defects and the addition of new features found to be necessary during production. It is expenditure on software development and maintenance in excess of that which would have been incurred if the product had been built exactly right first time.

The relationships shown in Figure 1.4 have been questioned. It is assumed that the cost of production of the software product is constant with respect to the quality level of the software. This may not be the case.

If differences in the quality level reflect differences in the performance, reliability, etc. of the software, there may well be a positive relationship between the cost of production and the quality level, but this should not change the relationship significantly.

Total quality-related costs (curves 1 and 2) are often subdivided into four groups:

- prevention costs: quality planning, employee training, supplier education, etc.
- appraisal costs: reviews, walkthroughs and other forms of testing
- costs of correcting defects discovered before acceptance
- costs of correcting defects discovered after acceptance which have to be borne by the developer

The cost-minimising quality level is sometimes described as the optimal quality level. We feel that this is misleading and prefer to reserve the term optimal quality level for use in models which include the revenue generated from sales, since this may be a function of the quality level.

There is as yet very little empirical evidence available for any of the relationships shown in Figure 1.4, and this can make it very difficult to convince cost-conscious management of the benefits which accrue from quality assurance. This problem is made more difficult because the cost of quality assurance activities (curve 1) such as appraisal and prevention are more easily estimated than the expected savings (curve 2). We suspect that as a result, in general, expenditure on quality assurance is sub-optimal, but we are biased.

It is a widely held view that most errors in large software systems are introduced in the early stages of the software development and that these errors are due to poor problem analysis and design. Quality assurance activities should prevent errors entering during these stages and also detect earlier some of those that do enter. In the case of errors prevented, the cost savings are difficult to estimate because it can never be known how many errors were prevented nor when they would otherwise have been discovered. The cost of preventing these errors from entering is not accurately predictable. Substantial cost savings can be made by earlier discovery of design errors and specification inadequacies, but again these are difficult to quantify.

It can be argued that in the longer term quality improvements might be reflected in a reduction in direct software development costs. It can for instance be argued that structured programming increases software quality and programmer productivity, thus reducing software development costs. It is anticipated that investment in more sophisticated software development tools, perhaps incorporated in IPSEs, will result in a better quality product at the same time as increasing programmer productivity.

If higher quality software allows the developer to increase the ratio of cumulative production volume relative to that of the cumulative production volume of its competitors, then this will, through the experience curve, allow the developer to reduce the cost of software production relative to its competitors and, in the longer run, this may be very important.

1.5 The motivation to undertake quality assurance activities

There are a number of reasons why a software developer might wish to undertake quality assurance activities, in addition of course to the desire to produce a good product, which can be the prime motivating factor but usually is not.

Potential legal liability if the software fails is becoming increasingly important. There are increasing numbers of high-visibility computer-based systems, such as banking and traffic control systems, which have the property that the users' use of them affects large numbers of people and the failure of the software component of such systems could result in very large total claims for damages against the user and the developer. Less spectacular claims could arise from the failure of any piece of software due to a defect. Any successful defence against such claims is likely to include showing that the developer acted as a reasonable and prudent person could have been expected to act when developing the software in question. This would include showing that everything that could have been done to prevent the defect occurring in the software had been done. One way of doing this might be to show that the software was developed using the best practice techniques embodied in the various standards. This implies that the developer had a good quality assurance programme. There is also the implication that the developer will have to preserve the documentary evidence of a satisfactory development process for the whole time that the software is in use in case it should be needed as evidence. Product liability insurance will increasingly become available, but it seems likely that this will only be given if the same high standards of quality assurance activities have been applied to the production process.

The user may insist that the developer has a satisfactory software quality assurance program. It used to be argued that this was really none of the user's concern because the software was only paid for once it had passed its acceptance test and if it did not work then the potential user had not lost anything. This is now realised to be a very superficial argument. If the software is delivered late, or not delivered at all, or delivered with less functionality than expected, there is at best a loss of competitive advantage and at worst lives may be lost and property destroyed. If the user is to have confidence in the product then substantial participation in the development process will be required, particularly in the development of a satisfactory specification and in a number of reviews. It thus seems wholly reasonable for the user to seek reassurance about the developer's ability to produce a satisfactory product.

The developer may adopt a quality assurance programme because it has been shown to be cost effective. It has already been argued that it could reduce costs both by preventing errors and by detecting them earlier than would otherwise be the case.

It may make good marketing sense to be seen to have a rigorous quality assurance programme. Users of other products expect them to be guaranteed, and there is no obvious reason for having a different expectation about software. It would be a good marketing strategy to offer guarantees with software. It would show confidence in the product, unlike the explicit disclaimers of responsibility for anything which might go wrong which sometimes accompany software products. A Japanese company is reported as having given a guarantee for the software provided for one of its personal computers, and this created a lot of concern that the practice might spread; so far it has not. If a software developer is able to offer a guarantee it demonstrates considerable confidence in the quality assurance programme that it has followed.

2   Software Development Life Cycle

2.1 Managerial aspects

If a project is to be said to have been successfully managed it must have been controlled. Project management involves more than simply allowing project personnel to discharge their duties as they see fit. Historically the lack of visibility of the software as it was being developed is said to have been one of the major problems encountered by managers attempting to control a software development project. In our view visibility and control are positively related and therefore a development process which maximises software visibility is desirable. There will be a price to be paid for this visibility in terms of the volume of documentation which has to be produced, and perhaps in terms of the timing and number of activities which have to be undertaken.

In general terms software project planning involves defining what is to be produced and, having done this, breaking down the work to be performed into tasks, determining the allocation of resources to perform these tasks, and the scheduling of these tasks. It follows that a schedule for the completion of the major tasks will be available very early in a project. An estimate must be made of the resources needed to complete the tasks which have been identified. We note in passing that this is very difficult and that research is continuing into ways in which it can be done accurately. It is pointless to complain about cost and time overruns if the initial estimates were never feasible; good estimation is essential for good quality. As the project proceeds it is important that progress is monitored against the original schedule. Records should be kept in order to learn from each project and improve the estimation process. As more data become available, the application of statistical methods should improve the accuracy of the estimates.

Quality, as has often been stated, has to be built into the software and it is important that the initial project plan provides adequate resources for this.

The steps necessary to control the quality of the output from an activity as a quality cycle have been described by Born (1986):

1. define the objectives of the activity
2. plan and schedule the tasks which must be performed to achieve the objectives
3. assign those tasks
4. perform those tasks
5. monitor and react to the performance
6. establish that the objectives were achieved

The steps in the cycle are paired in such a way that the first is used as a control on the second: 1 with 6, 2 with 5, and 3 with 4. In terms of a software product, for instance, this means that the acceptance test (6) will be based upon the requirements specification (1). The quality cycle can be applied hierarchically in the sense that it can apply to the whole activity, to a stage within the activity such as the preparation of the top-level design or to a single task within an activity.

It seems sensible for project management to use a model of the software development process in planning to which the quality cycle concept can be easily applied. It should be remembered that the existence of standards to be used in undertaking the activities has been assumed: these will cover all aspects of the work to be done, ranging from the specification of the format in which the objectives will be stated, through precise directions for the performance of the individual tasks, to the specification of audit procedures to ensure that the standards have been properly followed and procedures for following up any discrepancies. This last activity is the 'monitor and react' step (5) in the quality cycle.

It is important that management can periodically review progress made on the project and in the light of that review decide whether or not to continue with the project. Obviously, such a review can be arbitrarily held at any time but what is required is a development process which allows these periodic reviews to take place at times which are related in a logical way to the development schedule and the visibility of the software. One possibility would be to hold such a review at the completion of each major task if these could be performed sequentially.

In order to plan the development of a software project a model of the software development process is required. On the basis of the discussion so far this process should maximise the software visibility and also break the work to be done into tasks or stages which can be performed sequentially in such a way that:

- the quality cycle concept can be used to control the quality of the project, the stages and the individual tasks
- progress can be reviewed at the end of each of the stages and a decision made to continue with the project or not

Models of the software development process which break it down into such stages are known as software development life cycle models. It is important to be clear that the breaking down of an activity into its component parts does not in itself imply that these components are performed sequentially one at a time. Much of the argument about the use of the life cycle model to control quality centres around our ability to define a software development process in terms of activities which can be performed sequentially one at a time. Nearly all software development life cycle models contain similar stages based upon an idealisation of observations of the software development process up to the late 1970s and its rather arbitrary division into sequential stages based upon distinct different activities performed in those stages.

2.2 Description

Many computer systems involve the parallel development of software and hardware. Whilst recognising this, we shall concentrate on the development of the software. The software development process could be represented as a V diagram, as in Figure 2.1.

The loops shown on each of the stages are intended to show that the completion of the stage may involve several iterations. It is essential that a number of in-process reviews take place and these may be one reason for the iteration.

As one moves down the left arm of the V the output from each of the stages is verified against the output from the preceding stage. For instance the software specification will be verified by ensuring that it describes the functions to be performed by the software in the system design. Similarly, the top-level design will be verified by checking that if implemented the software would meet its specification.

As one moves up the right arm, the output from each stage is verified against the corresponding design or specification baseline. The software specification is used as the basis for the derivation of the acceptance test. The system specification should state what the system should do and is thus a sensible starting point when determining what tests the product should pass in order to convince buyers that it meets their expressed requirements.

Thus the V diagram emphasises the relationships between the decomposition process which is inherent in the design process, shown on the left arm of the diagram, and the integration of components during the building of the product, shown on the right arm.

Each stage ends with the establishment of a new baseline. A baseline can be thought of as the definition of a product at a particular instant. A

N.B

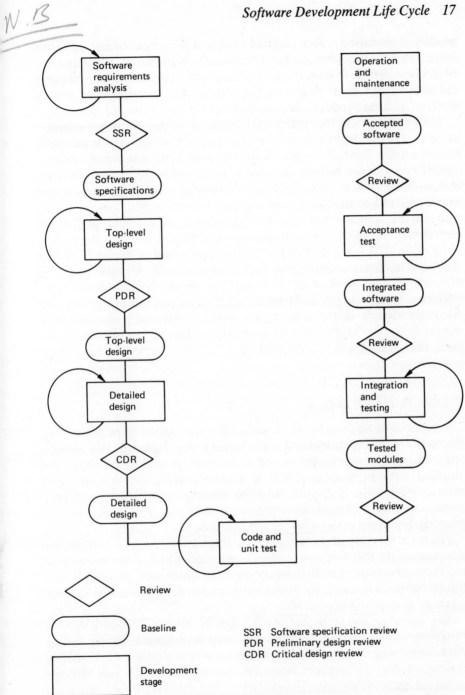

Figure 2.1. Software development life cycle diagram

baseline is established after a formal review of the output of a stage in the development of the software. Each stage ends with a formal review and the establishment of a new baseline. The baselines provide product visibility and the reviews provide the opportunity to decide whether or not to continue with the product's development.

The application of the quality cycle to this development process should be clear. The whole project starts with a specification, and this is used as a control on the finished system. Similarly, each stage has clearly defined objectives which can be used as a control on the output of that stage via the review. Within stages each task should have clear written objectives which can be used as a control on its undertaking.

It will be remembered that the software is being developed in an environment in which standards exist defining the way in which the work is to be done. The work undertaken during a stage will be reviewed during that stage to ensure conformance with these standards. All reviews will be of evidence that work was done and will usually be of documentary evidence. Common functions of all reviews include ensuring that this documentation is in the format laid down in the standards, that it is internally consistent, that it is understandable, that all the work has been done that should have been done and that the work has been done properly.

Requirements analysis stage

The purpose of this stage is to describe the functions to be performed by the software in a complete and unambiguous way. It should also identify any constraints on the system and make explicit statements about the required software quality. This is an extremely difficult task to perform satisfactorily and may require obtaining the user's reaction to prototype systems to ensure that all the user's requirements have been elicited and properly expressed in the software specification.

The main function of the software specification review is to consider the adequacy of the software requirements specification and, if the members of the review body are satisfied, to approve the documents produced. This formal approval is necessary before work can be officially allowed to begin on the next stage of the project.

The formal review is the last of a number of reviews. The work done in the preparation of the software requirements specification should already have been subject to a number of reviews, sometimes called internal reviews to distinguish them from the final review, which is sometimes called an external review. The customer, and perhaps other parties not related to the development team, will be represented at the final review. The terminology is based on the relationship of the people doing the reviewing to the development team. Unfortunately, the names are used inconsistently by different authors; internal reviews are also referred to as informal and the external review as formal, while others reserve the term formal review for a review which generates a report which is submitted to project management.

The approved document may be referred to as an allocated or functional baseline. The term allocated baseline is used to refer to a document which states the agreed allocation of functions to software and hardware components of the system, and functional baseline refers to a description of the product in terms of its functions. The terms are synonymous if a single computer program is being developed for an existing machine.

The review board's function does not extend to the correction of errors; its function is to identify them. The composition of the board will vary from project to project but should include the customer's representative (who might well be the chairperson), representatives from the development team, quality assurance personnel and representatives from the team undertaking the next stage of development, if different from those already represented.

Preliminary design stage

This is the design of the software architecture. The basic activity in this stage is to allocate the function of meeting each of the requirements to identified software components and to define the way in which these components will interact. It should be possible to take any requirement and find the software component which implements it or, starting with any software component, it should be possible to identify which requirement that component implements. The objective of this stage is to produce a set of software components defined by their function which, when combined in a particular way, will ensure that the system satisfies the software requirements specification. As part of this design process the control and data flows between these software components will have been identified, as will such things as local and global data structures.

Some sizing activity should take place to estimate memory requirements and processing time, and to ensure that any constraints on these in the software requirements specification can be met.

Once the functions of the various components of the system have been defined, it is possible to start making plans for testing them. The resources which will be required for testing can be identified, and the way in which the various software components can be tested to show that they meet their specification can be stated.

It should also be possible at this stage to produce some preliminary documentation, such as user manuals.

During this stage there will be a number of internal reviews which, in addition to such things as ensuring that the work was done in conformance with the standards, will ensure that traceability exists and that the design was undertaken to the appropriate level of detail. The standards will define the design methodology to be used and this will define the level of detail. It may be necessary to undertake the lower-level design work in certain areas in order to be confident that the top-level design can be implemented satisfactorily. The standards will also specify a number of review meetings or walkthroughs at which the emerging design will be examined and tested.

The in-process reviews of the test plan will be directed towards ensuring that there is adequate coverage of all software requirements.

The preliminary design review should ensure:

- that the design describes a system which when implemented will meet the software requirements specification
- that the test plan will satisfactorily test the software so that the user can have confidence in it if it passes these tests
- that the documentation being produced is adequate for its task

The design must also be feasible. There are a number of aspects to consider, most of which involve elements of judgement: for instance, is the human–computer interface satisfactory? Can the users be expected to fulfil their roles; for instance, a single user cannot operate a tracker ball, a key pad and a light pen at the same time. Is this the first system of its type and, if so, has sufficient allowance been made for this?

Detailed design stage

The object of this stage is to refine the top-level design by designing a fully detailed description of how the top-level software components can be implemented. This will usually involve further decomposition of the top-level software components into modules. In a good design each module will perform a single function. At the end of the process all the algorithms will have been identified, the data structures to be used will have been determined and the control flow will be known. There seems to be a consensus that in a good design the modules will:

- exhibit a high degree of cohesion and a low degree of coupling
- be of an appropriate size: a precise figure is difficult to give, but problems of understanding can arise if a module is too small or too big
- be easy to test: it must be possible to test every path through a module. The ease with which this can be done depends upon the control flow within the module. A good design, therefore, is one in

which the module has the simplest possible structure for its task. Unfortunately, even in a module with a simple internal structure the number of possible paths may be so large as to make testing very expensive

The method to be used to decompose the top-level software components and to design the modules will be specified in the company standards and the work done will be checked for conformance with this standard. The design of a module should be subject to some sort of review process as part of its development, since this is a highly cost-effective method of reducing errors. The detailed design of each module should be checked to ensure that it can meet any sizing and timing requirements that have been placed upon it. Any assumptions made when designing the module should be documented and the implications of any new ones investigated. The design should be reviewed to ensure that traceability has been maintained and that the design has been undertaken to the required level of detail.

Test specifications can be drawn up for each of the modules and for their integration; test cases (data) can be prepared and test procedures designed. Both black-box and white-box testing should be undertaken. Black-box testing will test a module's functionality but may not ensure that all paths in the module are exercised; white-box testing should be used to supplement black-box testing in an attempt to do this. The term coverage has been used to describe how close testing comes to this ideal. Coverage can be measured in several different ways.

The testing of software is a major part of the development process and plays a significant role in providing confidence that the software is fit for its purpose. It will take a significant fraction of the development budget. It follows that test plans, specifications, procedures and cases should themselves be 'tested' to ensure that they are satisfactory. As part of the development process, the test specification will be evaluated against the test plan and all aspects of the testing process including documentation will be checked for conformance with company standards. Test specifications should be reviewed to ensure adequate coverage and for consistency with the design documentation.

A draft of the various systems manuals should be produced at this stage. The critical design review will:

- check that the detailed design, if it were implemented, would satisfy the software requirements specification
- check that the detailed design was derived from the top-level design using the appropriate techniques
- check that sizing and timing estimates have been prepared, if appropriate, and that the software should meet any constraints imposed in those areas

- check that the test specifications provide adequate coverage of the software

Code and unit test stage

The object of this stage is to produce source code and object code versions of the modules which have been shown to implement correctly their specifications. This stage should also produce objective evidence of the unit testing and its results.

It is probable that coding and testing will be carried out in some order, the order being based upon the developer's view of the criticality of each module. Unless the development team are very lucky and/or very skilled, this will generate a series of changes which will affect the design and hence the coding of other modules.

Once the source module has been written it should be subject to some form of static analysis. It is very important to hold code inspections, walkthroughs and audits as coding proceeds. A code inspection is a review of the program code, usually against a checklist of factors to minimise the possibility that potential defects have been overlooked. A walkthrough is a structured evaluation of the code by project development personnel to ensure that it meets the module specification. Usually, the programmer will explain the code to the group which will attempt to detect any problems within it, the object being to ensure that the module meets its specification in a sensible way. A code audit evaluates the code against the company's coding standard, checking for format, comments etc. Obviously the evolving source program must be controlled during this process. It would be a waste of time to inspect/walkthrough/audit something which could be changed at the whim of the programmer. Once all the problems revealed by the process of evaluation have been corrected, object code should be produced, and the tests which were specified at the detailed design stage should be carried out. If any problems are found, they should be resolved and testing repeated.

At the end of this stage the review body will examine the evidence to satisfy itself that the work was done properly. It will also review the evidence of the testing process to ensure that it was carried out according to the test procedures. If satisfied on these issues and with the results of the tests, the review body will approve the tested modules as satisfying the specification.

Integration and integration testing

The object of this stage is to ensure that the tested modules work together as envisaged in the top-level design. There are a number of ways in which the tested modules can be integrated, the two extremes being top down and bottom up. However the modules are integrated, the basic approach is to integrate by adding one module at a time and testing the evolving aggregate rather than integrating all the modules and testing the whole program. Experience has shown what common sense suggests, which is that it is much easier to find the causes of any errors if one proceeds incrementally. For any large system integration, testing may require large amounts of special software such as stubs or test harnesses.

Integration test specifications will have been prepared and approved at the top-level design stage. The approach to be taken to integration will have been stated in the software development plan prepared and approved during the early part of the project. The tests are carried out as always in accordance with the approved test procedures and using approved test cases; these will probably have been prepared during the time that coding and unit testing was being undertaken. It might be noted in passing that the preparation of satisfactory test data can be a major undertaking. It is particularly important that a closed-loop system is in operation to handle defects revealed during integration testing and that regression testing is carried out. It is assumed for the purposes of this description that the whole system is tested at the end of the integration process.

The integration testing process will be reviewed to ensure that it was carried out properly; if it was, and the results were satisfactory, then the integrated software will be approved and may be presented for customer acceptance.

Acceptance test

The exact form of the acceptance test will obviously vary from purchase to purchase, but in general terms it will consist of a number of tests to demonstrate that the functionality and performance of the system is in conformity with the requirements, whilst ensuring that any stated constraints are satisfied. If the customer agrees that the results are satisfactory the product will be accepted. The process may involve the use of special software or other resources. A prudent developer will already have tested the software to ensure that it reaches at least the standard necessary for it to pass the acceptance test as part of the systems integration and test stage.

In practice, it may be very expensive to stage the acceptance tests and a preliminary review; a test readiness review is often held to ensure that the formal test procedures are satisfactory and to agree what should be done if the system fails a test. It may be sensible, given the set-up costs for these tests, to allow testing to continue after some sort of temporary repair. If this is to be allowed then the extent of retesting should be agreed and the change control process should be rigorously applied. Acceptance criteria should be reviewed and the customer should state what, if any, non-compliances with the specification would be tolerable and for what period of time.

The formal test procedures would usually require that the tests are performed by people independent of the development personnel. During this stage the testing should be monitored to ensure that:

- it is performed in accordance with the approved test specifications using the approved test procedures and cases
- it is performed on the approved versions of the code
- all reported defects are cleared and all retesting carried out

Once the tests have been carried out the results of testing will be reviewed. The test summary will be considered and the testing process reviewed to ensure that it was carried out properly.

2.3 Criticisms of the traditional software life cycle model

Criticisms of the traditional software life cycle model fall into several groups:

- It is based on old-fashioned software development methods. New approaches using automated techniques, object-oriented development or rapid prototyping do not fit easily within it. Life cycles for these techniques, with the properties of clearly defined stages, reviews etc., could be devised.
- Today's projects are of a scale and complexity which prevents the review process working properly.
- The traditional life cycle never did accurately represent the software development process.

We shall consider these points in more detail.

The software development life cycle model which has been presented is only one paradigm. There are others: Balzer (1985) advances one for automated software development which is likely to become increasingly important over time, as more and more automated development tools become available in response to economic pressure and theoretical advances (see Figure 2.2). The ideal form of the automated process involves specification capture and validation, followed by the automatic conversion of the specification into an efficient implementation. However, it seems likely that for some time into the future the conversion into an efficient implementation will require human assistance. We thus have a model in which a high-level specification is produced and translated into a lower-level specification which can be used as input to a process which generates a source code program.

This development paradigm can be refined. If the high-level specification

W.B

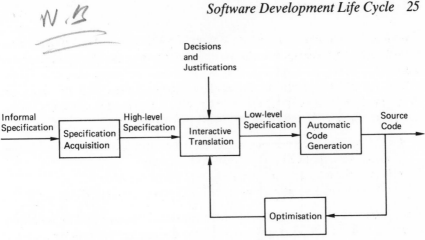

Figure 2.2. Initial automatic software development paradigm

can be executed, it can be used as a prototype which is of considerable assistance in the process of validating the specification. That is, checking that the specification really does describe what it was intended to. It is felt that deficiencies in the specification are a major cause of program main-tenance. If the process of implementing the specification were automated, then maintenance could be performed by modifying the specification and re-implementing it. There is a clear analogy here with the way in which maintenance currently involves changing the source code and re-compiling it.

The transformation from the high-level specification to the low-level one will be done by the application of a number of transformations to the specification. These transformations, their order of application and the reasons why they should be applied at that point, can easily be recorded. This record is called a formal development. We thus have the final version of the automated programming paradigm (Figure 2.3).

Balzer makes the point that there are two fundamental flaws in the traditional software development life cycle paradigm which are not present in the automated programming paradigm. The first flaw is that the process which converts the specification into an implementation is usually under-taken by humans in an informal way, and the documentation of that process may well not record the reasons why a particular method of implementation was chosen. It may be that the developers made their decisions on the basis of experience and were incapable of rationalising and articulating the reasons for their choices. In the automatic programming paradigm the human decision-making is fully reflected and recorded in the formal development.

The second flaw is that maintenance is usually performed upon the source code, which is likely to prove more difficult than performing it on the specification and re-deriving the source automatically.

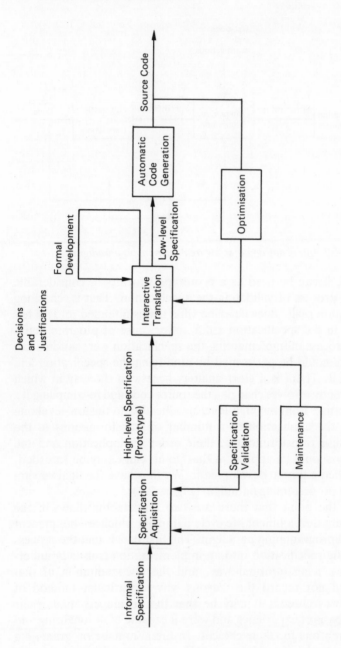

Figure 2.3. Final automatic software development paradigm

There seem to be two types of use of prototyping. The first is to produce a prototype of the user interface which is used in the process of requirements capture and validation and is subsequently discarded. This does not affect the life cycle model. The second use of prototyping is in the context of an incremental development approach, in which the prototype is intended to evolve into the final system. In this approach the top-level design of the system is completed and approved and the detailed design is undertaken to the point at which the interfaces between the modules can be fully defined and controlled. It may then be possible to proceed with the detailed design, coding and unit testing of modules independently, enabling the developer to test a working subset of the system in operation by only implementing certain modules. The implication is that some modules will be completed before the design of others is started and that the detailed design, coding and testing on different modules will be taking place at the same time.

This seems to be the essence of the argument put forward to support the third of the criticisms of the traditional software development life cycle, which was that it never did reflect the software development process. Software developers have always identified certain modules as critical and developed those first, even if there was no intention of producing a working prototype. This amounts to defining a priority ordering on modules and was done at the detailed design, coding and unit testing stages.

The second of the criticisms concerned the implications for the review process of the size and complexity of some present-day software projects. It is often the case that reviewers have enormous volumes of documentation to master. It seems unlikely that any individual could perform an adequate review of the technical issues raised in the documentation, given the time and skill constraints. From the developer's point of view, the length of time taken for the review process can cause project development problems; the project team members must do something with their time whilst waiting for the review to take place. If they continue working on the project, the review documentation will become out of date as more development work is done; if they do not continue working on the project, momentum is lost and ultimately productivity will be lower than necessary once work restarts on the project, because of the disruption. One suggestion is to have smaller, more frequent reviews, but it is not clear that this is a solution. For instance, it is not obvious that the top-level design can be reviewed by parts.

It is our feeling that the traditional life cycle model will very rapidly be supplemented by a number of others, each of which will lend itself to satisfactory software quality assurance activity. The difficulties involved in adequately reviewing work done may be much harder to resolve.

3　Software Quality Assurance Plans

3.1 Role of the software quality assurance plan

The user needs the software and has expectations of its quality which will usually be wider than the expectation that it will work. The user cannot take the attitude that if the software does not work it need not be paid for and that therefore there is no loss if it fails the acceptance test. There will be a loss of time and competitive advantage. The user is entitled to ask for an assurance that the software, when finished, will perform according to its specification.

The public may be affected by the user's use of the software. The user's possible liability for damages, should the public be harmed in some way by the malfunction of the software, reinforces the user's requirement that the software should be of suitable quality.

Quality is achieved by building it into the software; it cannot be added once the software has been developed. This implies that the relationship between software quality and the development process is known and that, by proper engineering of this process, a product of the appropriate quality can be produced.

The quality of the software as it is developed must be continually evaluated to ensure that it is satisfactory. This evaluation must be planned and documented. The planning of how the quality is to be built in and also how it is to be evaluated is recorded in the quality plan. This plan should be produced very early in the life of the software development project. It may not exist as a separate document but in this case it should be incorporated in some other document, perhaps a development plan. The software quality plan should give the user confidence that the product will be of the proper quality.

It must always be borne in mind that the nature of the application will determine the appropriate level of quality. Quality costs money and there will be an optimum level of quality for most applications. It is not worth buying more quality than is required.

To plan for and build quality into the software, the developer must undertake a number of activities. A complete set of software requirements must be established and maintained. These provide the standard against which the quality of the software is to be judged. Given the set of software requirements, a methodology for developing software to implement them can be engineered and implemented. The software can then be designed, built and tested using this methodology.

The quality of the evolving software product must be evaluated throughout its development. There are a number of activities involved in doing this. The requirements specification must be evaluated, both to ensure that the desired quality of the software product is clearly stated either explicity or implicitly and to ensure its technical adequacy. The software development methodology must be evaluated both as planned and as implemented. The evolving software product must be evaluated for quality. It is very important (and obvious) that some mechanism must exist, and be seen to exist, to feed back the results of these evaluations into the software development process and ensure that they are acted upon.

3.2 Content of the software quality assurance plan

The ANSI/IEEE Standard for Software Quality Assurance Plans states that such a plan should contain the following sections:

- purpose
- reference documents
- management
- documentation
- standards, practices and conventions
- reviews and audits
- configuration management
- problem reporting and corrective action
- tools, techniques and methodologies
- code control
- media control
- supplier control
- records collection, maintenance and retention

which are now considered individually and related to the process of building quality into software which has already been described.

Purpose

This states the specific purpose and scope of the plan. It names the software products that it covers and describes the use to which they will be put.

Referenced documents

A complete list of the documents referenced in the plan.

Management

The standard lays down three aspects that should be covered in this section: organisation, tasks and responsibilities. It is difficult to elaborate on this framework outside the context of a particular project.

Organisation

The management structure of a typical project is shown in Figure 3.1. It is important that the authority of the quality manager is at least as great as that of the project leader, and preferably greater. In many cases companies will draw the management structure charts to give this impression, but examination of salaries (and hence status) shows that the quality manager is really a fairly low-ranking management post. This can usually be interpreted as indicating a lack of real commitment to product quality by company top management.

The project leader is formally responsible for all aspects of software quality. Responsibility for quality control is delegated to all members of the development team.

Tasks

Assuming the prior existence of a comprehensive set of company standards, the chronological sequence of tasks which need to be performed includes:

- production of a preliminary software requirements specification; perhaps as part of the development of a system involving hardware and software
- preparation of a software configuration management plan, a software quality assurance plan and a software development plan which may or may not include the other two documents
- system requirements review
- system design review
- production of software requirements specification
- software requirements specification review
- production of a software test plan
- production of a top-level software design
- production of draft support documentation, e.g. user manuals, etc.
- top-level software design review
- production of software test description
- production of a detailed software design

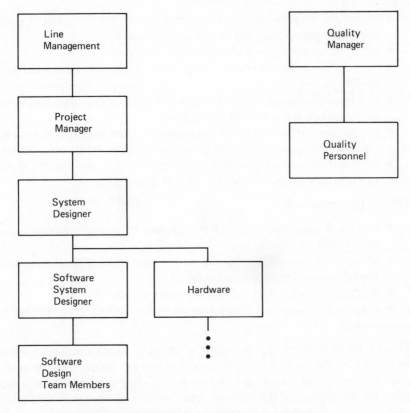

Fig 3.1. Management structure of a typical project

- detailed software design review
- production of software test procedures
- production of source code and object code for the code units
- testing of code units
- integration of software units
- testing of integrated software units
- systems integration
- systems integration testing
- acceptance testing

Responsibilities
The project manager and design/development team have primary responsibility for the quality controls applied during the development of the software project.

The quality manager will:

- define the responsibilities of quality personnel in the form of quality assurance procedures applicable to the project
- agree the quality plan with the project manager
- approve the plan of audits for the project which are to be carried out by quality personnel
- resolve any disagreement between the project manager and quality personnel on matters relating to quality
- review the activities of quality personnel to determine that the requirements of the quality plan and quality procedures are being satisfied
- review the contents of software standards, engineering codes of practice and quality procedures for adequacy and efficiency

 Quality personnel will:

- carry out planned audits of the project to assess compliance with quality objectives
- agree corrective action with the project manager for any discrepancies found and ensure that action is taken
- evaluate defect trends and take appropriate action
- refer any unresolved discrepancies to the quality manager for resolution

One would be looking, in this section of the plan, to see a real commitment to quality on the part of the company. Quality personnel must be seen to have authority and power. It is desirable that they should be independent from the developers of the software and they should have sufficient resources, authority and technical expertise to perform quality evaluation activities objectively and initiate corrective action, if appropriate.

Documentation

All the documentation relating to the development, verification, use and maintenance of the software will be listed. This will normally include:

- software requirements specification
- software design description
- software verification plan: this describes the methods used to verify that the requirements in the software requirements specification are implemented in the design and in the code, and that the code, when executed, meets the requirements expressed in the software requirements specification. These methods will include inspections, testing, analysis, etc.
- software verification report: this decribes the results of executing the software verification plan and includes the results of all reviews, audits, tests, etc.

- software standards and procedures manual
- user guides, operators' and programmers' manuals
- configuration management plan
- software quality assurance plan

This section may also include the software development plan. It will include details of the procedures by which each of the documents is approved. It should explain how the documents will be evaluated, what reviews will take place and the signatures required to authorise the documents.

Standards, practices and conventions

The developer will have designed and documented the process by which the software will be built. This expresses the methodology adopted. Work will be undertaken according to defined standards and in defined ways. These standards will be written down and used by the development team. Quality personnel will check that the work has been done in accordance with these standards. The standards encompassed in these documents will cover things as diverse as the contents and format of each of the documents produced during the development, the textual layout of the code, the reviews to be undertaken, the composition of the review board, the design methodology to be used to produce the software design, configuration management and testing.

This section of the plan will identify the standards, practices and conventions to be applied and state how it is proposed to ensure that the work is undertaken in accordance with these standards. The plan states that, at a minimum, there will be standards for documentation, algorithm description, coding and commentary.

Reviews and audits

This section of the plan will state which technical and managerial reviews will be undertaken and how they will be carried out. One would expect a schedule of provisional dates to be given for the major 'set piece' reviews, such as the software requirements specification review.

The ANSI standard suggests that the following would be a minimal set of reviews:

Software requirements specification review

This is held to approve the document defining the software requirements specification and it aims to check the adequacy of the requirements. At this review the project manager will be expected to state which evaluation activities have taken place during the preparation of the document. These evaluation activities will ensure that the preparation of the requirements specification was undertaken in accordance with the developers' codes of practice using approved tools and techniques. The document will have been checked to ensure that it conforms with the appropriate company standard.

The technical adequacy of the specification should have been evaluated to ensure that it forms the basis from which software of the desired quality can be developed.

The requirements specification document will have been checked for internal consistency, understandability and completeness.

It is increasingly being realised that it is important to ensure that the required quality aspects of the product are explicitly stated in the specification. It is not sensible to hope that software of the required quality can be produced without proper analysis of the required quality and its formal explicit statement. The adequacy of the quality aspects can be evaluated once they have been stated. Proper recognition of the desired quality aspects at the earliest possible stage is in everyone's interest.

To aid traceability it is helpful if each requirement has a unique identifier.

Preliminary design review
The purpose of this review is to approve formally the software top-level design document. As part of this process a summary of the quality evaluation activities undertaken during the top-level design will be reviewed. These will have included ensuring that:

- the design was produced in accordance with the developers' standards chosen to implement the selected methodology
- all necessary tasks were undertaken
- the top-level design is an adequate basis for future work
- the top-level design when implemented will satisfy any sizing and timing constraints
- the software top-level design document was produced in accordance with the company's standard and is internally consistent, understandable, complete and appropriately detailed

The design document will be checked to ensure that each of the requirements in the requirements specification can be traced to a part of the design. Forwards and backwards traceability is extremely important. It should be possible to trace each requirement forward from the requirements specification and see how it is implemented at each stage of the development process. Similarly, it should be possible to take any part of the software product at any stage in the production process and trace the reason for its existence back to the implementation of a particular requirement.

Critical design review

The purpose of this review is to approve the software detailed design document as a basis for further development work. As part of the process, a summary of the software evaluation activities undertaken during the detailed design phase will be reviewed. These will have included ensuring that

- the design was undertaken in accordance with the company's standards and is technically feasible
- all the necessary tasks were undertaken
- the detailed design was internally consistent, understandable, complete and appropriately detailed
- traceability is maintained through the top-level design to the software requirements specification
- unit test and integration cases have been prepared as part of the design and have been checked for consistency with the company's standards

Software verification review

The function of this review is to approve the test plan. It is an evaluation of the adequacy and completeness of the methods described.

Functional audit

This is held to verify that all the requirements in the software requirements specification have been met.

Physical audit

This is held to verify that the software and its documentation are internally consistent prior to delivery to the user.

In-process audits

In-process audits of a sample of the design are held to verify consistency of the design. Points which will be checked are consistency of code and documentation, consistency of design and functional requirements and consistency of functional requirements and test descriptions.

Managerial reviews

It is important that the execution of the quality plan is evaluated and there will be one or more reviews of this.

Configuration management

This section of the plan will cover configuration identification, configuration control, configuration status accounting, and configuration auditing. In many cases this section will simply refer to a separate plan, the configuration management plan, which will be discussed later.

Problem reporting and corrective action

This section will describe the system which ensures that software problems are documented and resolved. It should be a closed-loop system. All problems should be promptly reported, acted upon and resolved. Each problem should be capable of being tracked throughout the system.

Each problem should be analysed to determine its significance and causes and classified by category (such as requirements, design, coding, etc.) and priority. Trends in the problems reported should be identified.

For each problem or adverse trend discovered some corrective action and a target completion date should be identified. The appropriate level of management should be made aware of problems and adverse trends. Corrective action will be authorised and the activities undertaken will be documented. The corrective action taken will be evaluated to ensure that it solved the problem without introducing any new problems.

Management should monitor the status of all unresolved problems and be aware of any that have not been resolved by their target completion date.

Tools, techniques and methodologies

This section should identify the special software tools, techniques and methodologies employed that support quality assurance, state their purposes and describe their uses.

Code control

This is likely to be implemented in conjunction with a library function. The library receives and maintains copies of all software tools and documentation. The library will issue all material and ensure that the most recently authorised version is the one routinely available. Access to code files is controlled to ensure that no unauthorised use or modification takes place. The library will ensure that the correct version of software is submitted for testing.

Media control

This section will describe how the media are to be protected from unauthorised access or damage. One would expect to see details of storage arrangements that protected the media from harmful environmental conditions.

At least one back-up copy of the current configuration should be held safely.

Supplier control

It is important that externally developed software is of the appropriate quality: this section of the plan would state how it was proposed to ensure that this was the case. It would normally contain a form of words to the effect that subcontractors will implement a quality assurance program to the satisfaction of the main contractor who would have the right to evaluate the system. Software received from a subcontractor will of course be tested and evaluated before it is accepted.

It must be acknowledged that there are some cases in which little can be done to influence the quality of bought-in software. The classic case concerns computer manufacturer's operating systems. Anecdotal evidence suggests that in some cases the suppliers have been unwilling to provide any of the assurances concerning quality, support, etc. that purchasers have required. Software is supplied on a 'take it or leave it' basis, knowing that given the oligopolistic state of the market the potential purchaser cannot leave it. This situation where the supplier is in the dominant economic position is very difficult to handle and the problems that it creates appear incapable of easy resolution.

Records collection, maintenance and retention

Any successful project will undergo substantial maintenance over a long period and it is important to ensure that all the documentation necessary to undertake this quickly, efficiently and cheaply is going to be available when required. This documentation must be produced during development and retained. This section of the plan will identify who is responsible for ensuring that the appropriate documentation is produced and stored, and under what conditions.

4 Software Configuration Management

4.1 Managing the evolution of software

Software is often said to evolve, meaning that it is continually changing both during its formal development and usually during its in-service life. Software configuration management has been defined by Bersoff *et al.* (1980) as the discipline of identifying the configuration of a system at given times for the purpose of systematically controlling changes to this configuration and maintaining the integrity and traceability of this configuration throughout the system life cycle. It is thus founded upon the successive creation of baselines (as described in Chapter 2), each of which defines the product as it exists at that moment in time. Any change to an item appearing in a baseline must be controlled.

The integrity of the product is a measure of the extent to which it meets the needs and expectations of the software user. This implies that there must be a user input to the configuration management process to ensure that the evolving product is what the user/purchaser wants. The user should be motivated to play a role in the software development process because of the assurance that it provides during the development process that the software will meet their needs and expectations at the end of that process.

Configuration management has four component elements:

- Identification. The system can be defined in terms of its components. It must be possible to state exactly what components comprise the system at any moment in time.
- Control. The procedures for processing changes from whatever cause must be clearly defined early in the project.
- Status accounting. This is the recording, storing and reporting of all configuration identifications and all departures from the specified baselines. It is designed to ensure the traceability of changes to baselines and provide sufficient information about them for all purposes.
- Reviews to establish a new baseline. These define the configuration at an instant in time.

We shall consider the first three elements in more detail; the last was discussed in the software life cycle.

Identification

A configuration can be loosely described as a collection of related items. It is difficult in the abstract to say what items should be placed under configuration control in a software development project. One would expect to find requirements, specification and design documents, as well as the source and object code, test plans, other test documentation and probably many other project-specific documents. A software configuration item refers to a software entity which will provide defined functions and which has been explicitly placed under configuration control. It may be a program, an aggregation of programs, or a part of a program. Many factors have to be considered when choosing the initial set of software configuration items, including safety, complexity, susceptibility to change, and cost. The more software configuration items that are identified the greater the cost; selecting too few software configuration items, on the other hand, may lead to inadequate control over development and reduced product integrity. Inadequate control can result from the reduced visibility resulting from not having enough software configuration items. Management is interested in knowing where changes are being made; the implications differ if most changes are being made to a small number of areas, compared with a situation where changes are being made to all areas.

It has been suggested that systems should be designed in such a way as to produce a hierarchical relationship between their components because this will facilitate software configuration management. The relationship between the software configuration items can be shown graphically in what is known as the systems specification tree, which evolves with the configuration. The root of the tree is the total system as defined in the software requirements specification document. The next level in the tree is a functional decomposition of this into top-level software configuration items which are in their turn defined by specifications. The process of decomposing the software configuration items in this way continues throughout the design process, adding subsequent levels to the tree. Each item under configuration control needs to be uniquely identified, and a naming system based upon the relationship of the items in the tree structure is often suggested. The emphasis given to the importance of this type of structure because of its management implications can be carried to the extent of suggesting that the top-down functional decomposition design methodology is the only appropriate one. This is a mistake; the choice of software design methodology is a technical decision and should be made accordingly. The implication for software configuration management is only one of the factors which should be considered when making that decision.

There are problems in software configuration management which stem from the complex nature of software. For instance, it is necessary to identify all representations of the software and keep them consistent. Once it has reached the coding stage, the same software can be described by its specifications, its design documents, its source code listing and its object code listing. The source and object code may exist not only on paper but on tape and on magnetic disc, as well as in main storage. The problem gets worse if there are a number of versions of the software, say for different types of machine or operating systems. The potential for multiple versions of multiple representations demands rigorous software configuration management to prevent problems as the software evolves.

Configuration control

There are many reasons for change, which can be grouped in different ways. One of the more useful classifications is into discrepancies and requested changes. A discrepancy is the failure of the software to meet its requirements; it may be caused by things such as errors in the requirements, incorrect implementation of a requirement or the violation of the developer's standards. Requested changes tend to be improvements rather than repairs, although the distinction can break down if pushed too far. They may result from the discovery that a requirement cannot be implemented, from a desire to enhance the product by adding additional requirements, or from a desire to improve the product. Obviously, requests for changes can be made both by the developer and by the customer.

Configuration control provides the procedures necessary for proposing, evaluating, reviewing, approving and implementing changes to a baseline. Without these procedures, uncontrolled changes might cause more problems than they solve. Many organisations have a standard set of forms for these procedures which can be tailored to any particular project. All changes to a controlled item should be controlled using a formal procedure to obtain authorisation to make the change. The body which authorises changes is usually known as a configuration control board or a change control committee. Its membership and terms of reference will be defined in the configuration management plan which will be produced early in the project.

The configuration control board must be seen to have the authority to evaluate proposals and authorise the implementation of changes to the software product. This may mean that it has to be composed of the most senior representatives of all parties involved. In order to evaluate proposals the board members must be capable of understanding technical issues. These requirements sometimes lead to the establishment of a hierarchy of boards. A top-level board composed of senior people makes all the major decisions but delegates power to a lower-level board to make the day-to-day decisions. In practice it has often been found to be most effective to have one person on the board making the decisions based upon the advice of the other members. Democratic decision-making is not an obvious requirement for a configuration control board.

It is important for the board to be seen to respond rapidly to change proposals; failure to do this may result in project participants perceiving the board as a bottleneck and attempting to circumvent its authority. It is good practice to distribute the minutes of each meeting to all project personnel so that they know what the board is doing.

As part of the preparation of a change proposal, all persons likely to be affected by the proposed change should be notified and their views sought. When a change proposal is made to the configuration control board, it should be supported by all the information that will be needed to make a decision. This will include:

- the reason for the change and perhaps a discussion of the alternatives including the consequences of not making the change
- details of the proposed change
- the financial implications of making the change
- the effect on project timescales
- the effects of the change on the software product and thus on the contract and the relationship with the customer
- the implications of the change for other parts of the system
- the retesting required if the change is implemented

The consideration given to each of these items will probably vary with the type of change, that is whether it arises from a discrepancy report or a request for change. Not all discrepancies need to be fixed. In practice, the customer may feel that the discrepancy does not detract from the usefulness of the product sufficiently to be worth the cost of fixing it and a waiver may be issued. A discrepancy report can only be cleared in one of two ways, either by the issue of a waiver, or by the implementation of a change to fix the discrepancy. A change request can be cleared in one of two ways: it can be disapproved or it can be implemented.

The implementation of change needs to be carefully controlled. The configuration control board must ensure that a document authorising the change is delivered to the appropriate members of the development team. The change will be made, tested and, if found satisfactory, the changed software will be accepted. The completion of the change will be notified to all members of the development team and this will clear the discrepancy report or change request. In the case of changes to code it is important to test not only the changed code but also any other code which could have been affected by the change. There are many instances of changes to code having had unexpected effects on other parts of the system.

Configuration status accounting

This provides the mechanism for the recording, storing and reporting of all events in the development of the software. It enables the current status of the configuration to be ascertained and provides a way of tracing its history. It obviously poses hideous problems of data capture since it is not always clear at the time what information will be needed later. It is important to record when events occurred, as well as the details of the events themselves.

Experience has shown that it is also important to record information about the development environment where relevant; key features which need to be known include exact details of the hardware, operating systems and utilities, such as compilers, which were used during development. In the case of systems with a very long life, the inability to reproduce this development environment may make maintenance very difficult.

The current status of the configuration will be given by the identification of all the items in it, the status of any proposed changes to these items and the extent to which any approved changes have been implemented.

It seems likely that two types of report will be made. There will be a number of routine regular reports which are essential to the smooth running of the project; these include baseline status reports and the reports on the status of change requests and discrepancy reports. There will also be *ad hoc* reports for various purposes such as management decision-making. The configuration status accounting function can be thought of as a management information system.

Configuration management involves the storage, retrieval and updating of large amounts of information which is said to be held in a library. The successful undertaking of the library function is essential to successful configuration management, and the procedures for the operation of the library should be defined early in the project. The activities undertaken by the library will vary from organisation to organisation. In general, one would expect the library to be responsible for storage-related operations, such as the naming of the software configuration items and the physical storage of all software and related documents such as specifications, test documentation, all change proposals and related documentation, etc. This responsibility includes the security and safety aspects of storage and the storage of back-up copies of the material. The material must be stored in the correct environmental conditions and provision must be made periodically to review and renew the material if the medium on which it is stored is likely to deteriorate.

Retrieval-related operations for which the library would be responsible include the production of master and working copies of software. Working copies of software items are supplied to programmers authorised to change them. The library will supply controlled items for testing. Software supplied to customers will be provided by the library, which will keep records of the versions supplied to each customer in order to be able to notify them of any updates. The library may also be responsible for the notification of changes to controlled items to interested parties.

4.2 Software configuration management plan

Management should ensure that each software development project has a written statement of how software configuration management is to be implemented. This will include a description of the organisation involved and the responsibilities of each of its members, as well as the procedures to be used. This information is often contained in a configuration management plan prepared early in the project. ANSI (1983) identifies the essential items that should appear in a configuration management plan and recommends a plan that includes the following sections:

- introduction
- management
- software configuration management activities
- tools, techniques and methodologies
- supplier control
- records collection and retention

Much of the material in this plan, and indeed the format and content of the plan itself, could be covered in the developer's standards, and one would expect to see references to these, where applicable, in the plan rather than lengthy descriptions.

Introduction
This section contains four subsections: purpose, scope, definitions and acronyms, and references. This section is used to provide what is essentially background information and is often very brief. It does little more than identify the project to which software configuration management is to be applied. The extent to which software configuration management is to be applied is stated: it is expensive, and small, simple projects may not require the same type of control system as other larger, more complex ones.

Management

This section includes subsections concerning organisation, software configuration management responsibilities, interface control, software configuration management plan implementation, and applicable policies, directives and procedures. This section describes the organisational structure which will implement software configuration management. It is likely to reflect the structure of the developer's organisation and may include a hierarchy chart. One would expect to find the major elements of this structure, their relationships, their responsibilities and the source of their authority stated. It will identify the configuration control board and the library function. The provision to be made for software configuration management, after the development of the software, should be addressed.

The interface control subsection, if applicable, describes how interface specifications and the interface between the hardware and software shall be controlled. Particular attention should be given to the problems which arise if different versions of the software, and if any particular piece of software is dependent upon particular pieces of hardware.

The major milestones in the implementation of the software configuration management plan should be identified. These include such things as the establishment of the configuration control board, a schedule for software configuration management reviews and the establishment of various baselines.

The applicable policies, directives and procedures subsection describes in detail the way in which software configuration management will be undertaken for a project. It will include:

- program naming conventions and the use of standard headers for modules to ensure consistency
- identification of documents, media and files
- the releasing of software and documents
- the operation of the configuration control board
- the operation of the change control process
- the documents to be used in software configuration management

Software configuration management activities

This section has subsections covering the four elements of software configuration management which have already been discussed: identification, control, status accounting and reporting, and audits and reviews.

The subsection dealing with *identification* will identify the baselines and the items which are included in them. It will state the review and approval procedure necessary to establish the baseline. The labelling, numbering and cataloguing procedures for all software code and documentation will be stated so that there can be no uncertainty about the conventions to be used on the project.

The subsection dealing with *configuration control* will clearly state the authority for change approval. Most software configuration control systems classify changes in some way. For instance, it is often useful to distinguish changes which affect customer-approved products from those which do not and to require different approval processes for each type of change. All of the steps to be followed when processing change proposals and discrepancy reports will be stated in detail. The role of the configuration control board will be stated and its powers laid down. The method of selecting the members of this body should be given. One would expect to see a definitive statement of the factors to be used to evaluate proposals for change. The library control procedures might also be formally stated in the subsection.

The subsection concerned with *configuration status accounting* will set out what information is to be collected, how it is to be collected and stored. It will also state what regular reports are to be produced and what facilities will be provided for *ad hoc* reporting.

The subsection concerning *audits and reviews* will define the software configuration management role in the various audits and reviews which take place during the life cycle and identify the software configuration items involved. The procedures to be used to identify and resolve problems during these audits and reviews should be stated.

Tools, techniques and methodologies
This section is used to identify and describe the use being made of these things to support software configuration management. They may be proprietary products or have been developed in house.

Supplier control
This section details the action to be taken to ensure that suppliers implement a defined and satisfactory standard of software configuration management.

Records collection and retention
This section will identify the material to be retained, the storage method to be used and the period for which the material will be kept. This task is often treated casually, although attitudes are changing with the rapidly growing awareness of the desirability of applying statistical analysis to all aspects of the software development process and the need for information from past projects in order to be able to do this.

The configuration management plan should be written in such a way that it is easily understood by all project personnel. It is the project manager's responsibility to ensure that all personnel are aware of its contents and follow them.

4.3 Computer-aided software configuration management systems

Configuration management involves the storage, retrieval and updating of enormous volumes of information. The updating is in part the end product of change control processing and, amongst other things, involves notifying all interested parties of the proposed changes and seeking their views. To make this possible records must be kept of the relationship between software items and their owners/users.

Many software configuration management activities can be performed more easily and efficiently with computer assistance since they involve a lot of basically simple tasks which are very prone to error when undertaken by humans. Much of the library and change control functions can be automated and access to stored information controlled using computer-based systems. Many of the IPSEs currently being developed have facilities for automating most aspects of software configuration management and are designed to ensure that project staff cannot work outside the configuration management system. There are currently many systems available which perform some subset of the configuration management activities. Many companies have experimented with in-house systems based around database packages. Anecdotal evidence suggests that this is a non-trivial undertaking and should be carefully costed.

The ideal system would be one in which the project software development system automatically generated the necessary control and management information from the development process itself. Program support libraries probably represent the current state of the art in this respect and fall short of the ideal. They are a widely used aid for controlling software at the coding stage. They should be controlled by a librarian who must not be one of the programmers working on the project.

Project information such as documentation, source code, object code and configuration management information is held electronically. Access to it is controlled by giving users different access privileges to the stored information. Most users will be very restricted in what they can change. For instance, it seems sensible to allow all programmers to read interface and other design information if they wish, but to limit a programmer's power to change things to items that he or she has specific authority to change. There should be no circumstances in which a programmer needs unrestricted power over information. The system usually records in a log the changes made by anyone to any item. In this type of environment it is difficult for anyone to work outside the control of configuration management.

Obviously, not all project information will be held in machine-readable form: a program support library also includes documents and other material in an external library, as well as a number of procedures in addition to the machine-readable information.

It is sometimes useful to think of a program support library as being composed of four mutually exclusive areas:

- a working area holding non-approved information, for instance programs under development or modification
- a controlled area holding information which has been approved and is subject to configuration control. If a modification to an item in this controlled area has been approved then a copy of the item is placed in the working area of the person with the authority to modify it. Once modified the item cannot be replaced in the controlled area until it has been approved as having been correctly and satisfactorily modified. The procedure for approval and re-entry will have been defined in the configuration management plan
- an area holding configuration management information and also used as a working area by the librarian
- an area holding all released versions of documentation

A minimal program support library will provide centralised facilities for holding authorised versions of each software configuration item and hold the data needed for the proper development and control of those items. In general program support libraries can be used to support three areas of activity: code development, management of software development, and configuration control.

A maximal program support library will contribute substantially to configuration control by controlling access to all data in the library and providing a mechanism for making approved changes to that data. It may conduct some of the change proposal processing. It will provide automatic change tracking and reporting facilities and go a long way towards ensuring the consistency of the various representations of the software and any other documentation. It can also provide automatic program and document reconstruction.

The use of computer-aided configuration management has certain advantages. It will ensure standardisation of record keeping across the project; for instance, each module usually has a standard header containing information about itself. Any attempt to enter software into the controlled area of the program support library without this standard header will fail.

It is hard to conceive of major projects not using computer-aided configuration management systems because of the difficulty and cost of undertaking the task manually. Computer-aided configuration management systems undoubtedly provide facilities for greater visibility and control during development. The integration of text processing, graphics and electronic mail facilities into these systems can result in substantial increases in efficiency and reductions in overall cost.

The main disadvantages of these systems are the initial cost and potential vulnerability. The initial cost of a minimal program support library can be quite small as a percentage of total project costs. The vulnerability problem is serious; the configuration management system is essential to the successful development and maintenance of the software, and the project cannot continue for long without it. It follows that the system must be designed to ensure that there are no circumstances which would result in its being unavailable for long periods of time or which would corrupt the data held in the program support library and prevent its successful reconstruction once the corruption had been discovered.

5 Design Reviews

5.1 Activity of design reviews

The reduction of rework costs is one of the objectives of software quality assurance. To do this one must either prevent errors or find them as early as possible. The relative cost of correcting errors increases rapidly as the length of time between occurrence and detection increases. Error prevention is the most cost-effective approach, but error detection techniques such as audits and reviews are probably more widely used than error prevention techniques such as modelling and prototyping.

Terminology has not yet been standardised in this area and some confusion exists in the literature as to the meaning of names such as technical review, design review, inspection, walkthrough and audit. The names are used inconsistently by different authors and the meaning must be interpreted from the context. ANSI/ASQC (1978) gives the following definitions:

Technical review (design review). The formal review of an existing or proposed design for the pupose of detection and remedy of design deficiencies which could affect fitness-for-use and environmental aspects of the product, process or service and/or for identification of improvements of performance, safety and economic aspects.

Product quality audits. A quantitative assessment of conformance to required product characteristics.

Inspection. The process of measuring, examining, testing, gauging or otherwise comparing the unit with the applicable requirements.

It has been traditional to classify reviews as technical or managerial; managerial reviews are related to management plans and project progress. Project management needs to have an evaluation of the technical output from the development team. To get a reliable evaluation it must be done by people other than those who produced the output. A technical review is a form of testing of a software configuration item and is classified according to the product being reviewed.

The minimal quality plan requires four reviews, two of which, the preliminary design review and the critical design review, are relevant to

49

this chapter. It must be borne in mind that there will have been reviews during the development of the material in each stage, as well as a final formal review at the end of each stage. The form of the review is not specified. Walkthroughs, inspections and audits are all forms of the review process and a choice must be made between them. The final design review is almost always an inspection.

A walkthrough is the presentation of material by the producer of that material to a selected audience the members of which have usually not spent long preparing for the walkthrough. The audience ask questions and point out problems as the presentation proceeds.

An inspection is a method of assessing material against its requirements using a specific set of criteria. A group of people meet to comment upon material which they have previously examined in depth: an inspection demands a great deal of preparatory work by the participants. There is a clearly defined procedure to be followed before, during and after the meeting. All inspections have some form of checklist or agenda which is used to structure the meeting and the participants' preparation. It has been found that two hours is the maximum useful length of time for a meeting, so more than one meeting may be necessary to cover the material. It has also been suggested that two two-hour meetings is a sensible maximum for a day's effort. Each member of the group has a particular role to play. The comments of the inspectors are formally recorded and acted upon.

The documentation produced by a formal technical review should always include a summary report for management stating what was reviewed and by whom, and their conclusions. A technical review issues list will be generated containing any comments which the inspectors wanted to have drawn to the team members' attention.

Formal design reviews may have a number of objectives:

- increasing project productivity by detecting errors early, thus reducing rework time and possibly decreasing the time which needs to
  be spent testing
- improving the quality of the software
- informing (educating) other members of the team about developments. This improves productivity by reducing errors caused by
  ignorance and makes the team more able to cope with the problems
  caused by loss of staff
- marking the completion of a stage in the development of the software
- producing more maintainable software. The chain of reasoning is that
  for software to be reviewed the reviewers must be able to understand
  it. It must therefore be well documented. The review thus forces the
  developer to produce documentation which might not otherwise have
  been produced until the end of the project, at which point resource

constraints might have reduced its quality. In addition, of course, the review process will increase the understanding of the software being developed

5.2 Structure of design reviews

To obtain the maximum value from a review it must have explicit objectives and a systematic method of reviewing the material. The participants in a formal review must play specific functional roles and in some cases this may mean that one person can play more than one role. The number of participants is probably a reflection of the importance of the review and the cost of staff time. In most types of review it is possible to identify the roles of review leader, recorder, producer and reviewers. Reviewers may be users, maintainers, quality controllers, specialists with knowledge of the application or specialists with knowledge of the design methodology. Exactly who the players of the reviewers' roles are will depend upon the application and the particular review.

The review leader is responsible for the review process. This involves ensuring that the review is properly planned, conducted and followed up. The recorder is responsible for collecting all of the information necessary to produce the technical review isssues list. This function is more complex than simply minuting the debate. In order to resolve disputes which may arise later concerning the recorder's work, it may be sensible to keep a verbatim record of the meeting, perhaps by tape-recording it. The producer of the item being reviewed is responsible for ensuring that all the other participants have all the information they need to carry out the review and for correcting any errors which may have been found. In a walkthrough, the producer would be expected to present the material to the meeting. This role requires considerable skill in the presentation of material at the correct pace and level. In an inspection, the producer would be expected to respond to the points raised by the reviewers. The reviewers should consider the design from the viewpoint of their particular skill or requirement. At the preliminary design review, the user may be the representative of the final user of the system; at the critical design review, where the individual modules are being reviewed, the user may be the designer of the modules on the other side of the interface. The user has to ensure that the item being reviewed will do what is expected of it and is thus responsible for maintaining product integrity. The quality controller's role includes responsibility for ensuring that the item being reviewed meets the standards laid down for it and that subsequent to the meeting all the items on the technical review issues list are cleared.

The review leader is responsible for planning the review. This is often, in practice, a difficult task. Consider the apparently simple task of setting a date for the review. It must take place as soon as possible after the work to be reviewed has been completed. If there is too long a delay, then project management has to make the decision whether to go ahead with the next stage of the development and take the risk of perhaps having to discard the work if the review, once it is actually held, discovers major architectural problems. The alternative might be to suspend work on the project and temporarily re-allocate the team members. On the other hand if the review is scheduled too early, then it may be a review of an incomplete product. This is usually a waste of time; it is often unclear whether problems exist because of the design or because it is incomplete.

The selection of participants is done on the basis of their competence to review the aspects of the software which the review has been scheduled to cover. There are many sources of complications in this task. It is very difficult to convince the people whose work is being reviewed that *they* are not being reviewed at the same time. The producer has a natural tendency to see criticism of the design as personal criticism and to react defensively. This reaction is counter-productive, but avoiding it may involve reducing the producer's motivation to do a good job. The producer must not feel threatened by the choice of reviewers. This can be difficult to do: good managers have informal channels of communication which they use to check on the information they receive from various reports. The inclusion of people as reviewers who are known to the producer to be part of these informal channels can cause problems. The review leader may not have the same knowledge of these channels as the producer; he may select such people in error or may be guided by management to select them when attempting to identify people with the appropriate skills.

Having scheduled the review, the review leader distributes copies of the material to be reviewed to the selected participants. It is also sensible to give the reviewers a clear set of guidelines (a checklist) detailing the most common errors in the type of item being reviewed and instructions on how to detect them. The reviewers then prepare for the meeting by studying the material they have been given, trying to understand it and to find errors in it. Without proper preparation on their part the review will not be very effective.

The review meeting will be conducted in strict accordance with the agenda. This may or may not require the producer to present the material being reviewed. The reviewers will ask questions of the producer to clarify their understanding of the material and will point out possible errors or raise other issues that they feel might be relevant. Any errors which are recognised as such and any other issues which seem to be significant are entered on the technical review issues list. It is general practice to attempt to classify these issues on a scale ranging from very serious (a major design error) to trivial. If a very serious error is found, then the review may be terminated; otherwise the review continues, the object being to find as many errors as possible.

It is important for the review leader to keep the discussion strictly to the agenda and ensure that no attempt is made to find solutions to the errors discovered. The function of the review is to find errors. It should not be allowed to correct them since this can waste a lot of time. It is the development team's task to correct the errors.

If errors have been found during the review it must be decided whether the item should be reviewed again once the errors have been corrected or if it can then be accepted without a further review. It is always prudent, but expensive, to require another review. One of the functions of the review is to provide confidence in the quality of the product at this stage in its development. If no errors have been found the product can be accepted.

It has already been suggested that the review should produce two reports: a summary report for management, and a technical review issues list containing points which require attention. Both reports should be lodged with the project librarian. It is helpful if the reports can be made available quickly. The reason for separating the reports is to reinforce the point that it is the *product* which is being reviewed, not the development team members; it is felt that giving management a list of the problems found would encourage them to use the review to appraise team members. In practice, of course, if management want to see the issues list they do. They will certainly need to be told of the timescale for the resolution of any issues.

In addition to management and the development team, whose interest in and use of the reports should be obvious, the final customer and the software quality assurance organisation have an interest in them. The final customer will use the report to appraise the quality of the software as it is being developed and to measure the progress being made by the development team. The software quality assurance organisation should use the report to evaluate both the software and its development process. The errors discovered indicate areas where the development process could be improved; perhaps the developer's standards are inadequate. Errors which escaped detection, but were subsequently discovered, indicate areas where the review process could be improved. The review guidelines should be changed to incorporate instructions on how these errors can be detected for use in future reviews. The software quality assurance organisation may also be responsible for ensuring that all the issues raised by the reviewers are cleared.

Criticisms of the way design reviews are sometimes currently held often include the following:

- an enormous volume of documentation has to be mastered by the reviewers
- inadequate time is allowed to master the documentation: reviewers are often expected to continue with their normal tasks and fit in the preparation for the review as best they can, usually in their own time
- reviewers are often not given clear responsibility for reviewing aspects of the design for which their skills fit them. They may thus feel responsible for reviewing the whole of the material and skim it in the hope of finding errors

Parnas and Weiss (1985) report a reviewing technique which can meet some of these criticisms. It is based around a technique in which each reviewer has to answer specific questions about the design which are related to his/her specialist skills. This approach ensures that reviewers concentrate their effort in areas where they are most likely to discover problems and thoroughly understand the material being reviewed. This approach is promising, but more experience with it will be necessary before its usefulness can be properly judged.

It is perhaps worth stating that these criticisms can also be met by organising the reviews properly and ensuring that sufficient resources are devoted to them.

5.3 Review topics and checklists

The following lists of questions are examples of those which could be asked by the reviewers.

Preliminary design review

Is the decomposition of the design appropriate for this stage?

Does the design represent a system which is capable of meeting the requirements as set out in the software requirements specification?

Have all the requirements been allocated to software items?

Do the test plans represent a systematic and logical approach to the testing of the software?

Do the test plans appear to test the software sufficiently thoroughly for the user to have confidence in it?

Does the design facilitate effective testing?

Does the design facilitate maintenance?

Have the test specifications been produced and approved?

Is the required test and support software available and has it been approved?

Is the design technically feasible?

Does the design demand hardware performance which is close to specification limits?

Does the design utilise most or all of the specified hardware capacity?

Does the design allow for future expansion and likely changes to the system?

Is the documentation which has been produced adequate for its purpose?

Critical design review

Does the design represent a system which will satisfy all of the requirements?

Has the detailed design been derived from the top-level design using the appropriate techniques?

Does each module correctly implement the functions required of it?

Does each module have a high degree of cohesion and a low degree of coupling?

Is the design of each module as simple as possible?

If necessary, have sizing and timing estimates been prepared and does the system meet any relevant constraints imposed in these areas?

Do the test specifications provide adequate coverage of the software?

Has proper provision been made for error handling?

Are there any interface problems either with hardware or software?

Are all the data structures initialised properly?

Do the algorithms work with boundary values?

If appropriate, have any synchronisation problems been identified and properly dealt with?

Does the design depend upon any assumptions made about the system which have not been explicitly stated?

6 Design

6.1 Introduction

Many projects have discovered to their cost the undesirable consequences of allowing software development staff to skimp the early stages of the software life cycle in order to get on to the more 'exciting' programming parts. The cost, in real terms, has been that of increased development time caused by error correction. Errors, like contagious diseases, are harder and more costly to eradicate the longer they are allowed to survive and spread. Greater care over specification and design is the only way of improving matters. Errors cost less to repair if they are picked up early; they cost nothing to repair if they are not made in the first place. Quality control is concerned with the detection and eradication of errors at the earliest possible moment in the software life cycle. As the Electrical Engineering Association publication *Establishing a Quality Assurance Function for Software* (EEA 1983) puts it, 'Quality can only be achieved by building it in from inception; it cannot be added at a later stage.'

Inception means the point at which the software requirements are specified, following on from there to the different levels of design. Quality control at these design stages will reap undoubted dividends in the faster production of working software. In this chapter we look at some of the issues involved.

6.2 Requirements specification

Objectives

A survey of US aerospace contractors, mentioned in DTI (1985), revealed that not only was inadequate requirements definition considered by 97% of project managers to be their major problem area, but that all other major problem areas were related to this same aspect. The quality of a requirements specification is thus of crucial concern.

Part of the problem is undoubtedly the fact that the requirements specification has to act as the interface between two parties that are often opposites: a user, who is looking for a statement of what the software will provide, and a developer, whose concern is that requirements define what is to be developed. The two parties may also speak a different 'language', with the user dealing in terms related to the application of the software whilst the developer is concerned with its implementation: this means that both the contents of, and the rationale behind, the requirements specification need to be addressed.

A good starting point, then, is to consider the overall *objectives* of a requirements document. (In this context the term 'document' may include both paper-based and machine-based material.) The list given by Heninger(1980) provides a useful basis for discussion. A requirements specification should aim to:

Specify external behaviour only
The requirements specification is not a design document. Other than at the relatively superficial level of allocating tasks between hardware, software and humanware, it should concentrate solely on the 'what' of the project, not on the 'how'.

Characterise acceptable responses to undesired events
A major subset of the 'what' is the 'what not' – that is, the events that are to be regarded as exceptions (or fault conditions), and the actions (the 'what') to be taken by the system when such conditions arise. All of which presupposes that another part of the 'what' is that of detecting that an exception condition exists.

Specify constraints in the implementation
Although eschewing design details, it is necessary at this point to consider any particular limitations that may influence design – such as required performance, for instance.

Be easy to change
This document is to form the first baseline for the project, with all other system documents being derived from it and, we hope, consistent with it. But refinement is an essential aspect of requirements definition particularly when, for instance, software is under development in a new problem area. Through techniques such as prototyping, requirements will only fully emerge as development proceeds. Changeability is therefore essential.

Serve as a reference tool
The basic question posed at all future stages of the project will be: 'does this (whatever) conform to the stated requirements?' Thus the requirements specification has to be in a form suitable for its use as a reference tool.

Record forethought about the life cycle of the system

Recourse will regularly be made to the requirements for the purposes of compliance. When divergences occur, either the design or the requirement must change. If the requirements specification includes a record of 'why' as well as 'what', the decision about which to change can be more readily assessed.

Content

By implication, our objectives for requirements specification lead on to both the design philosophy for such a document and, of course, to its content.

The document should provide detail in the following respects:

System functions

How the system should appear to the user in terms of individual functional elements. It is important that each be separately identified to facilitate tracing through the subsequent software design.

Correctness

Such things as accuracy of numeric outputs, search criteria on database accesses.

Reliability

Levels of availability throughout a working period such as a month, or a year.

Performance

Workloads that the system is required to handle, and necessary response times. If any doubt exists concerning the difference between functionality and performance, simply consider the case of a computer-controlled cardiac monitor. The functional requirement might be to sound an alarm when the monitored heart stops beating; the performance requirement might stipulate that the alarm be sounded within 0.1 of a second. Functionality alone would be of limited benefit!

Security

Required provision to guard a database, for example, against accidental or malicious access.

Usability

Requirements regarding the user interface to the software. To take an extreme example, a software system could meet the functional requirements but actually be unusable because it conducted its dialogue with the operator in a foreign language. As with performance, both types of requirement must be specified.

Maintainability
Stipulated requirements in terms of such areas as design approach, development methodology, use of standards. Note that this is not encroaching on decisions about design and development, but stating that those aspects must be tackled in a way that ensures ease of software maintenance at a later date.

Flexibility
Any requirements regarding future development of the software, e.g. capability to handle increased data volumes without change, or expand the content of a database.

Interoperability
Any need for the software to operate together with other software systems.

In addition, various umbrella criteria for the specification of a requirements document can be identified:

Requirements must be explicitly stated
This may not happen for a multiplicity of reasons: for instance, the customer may think that the requirement is obvious, or it may be considered to be implied by other stated requirements.

Requirements must be individually identified
It should be possible to trace them through the subsequent levels of software design – but this is hard work. It means, for instance, that interdependencies between individual requirements cannot simply be rolled into global statements but must also be individually specified. Short cuts are very tempting, but must be avoided.

Requirements must be testable
How else is it possible to say with any confidence that the requirements have been met? It should be possible from the definition of requirements to state how each requirement will be tested and for acceptance criteria to be outlined.

Requirements must be complete
Again, there are any number of reasons why this may not be the case: a requirement may have been overlooked; it may not even be known.

Requirements must be unambiguously stated
If the 'I thought it meant ...' syndrome is to be avoided there must be no doubt about the meaning of any requirement.

Even the few problem areas mentioned above should be sufficient to leave the reader with no illusions concerning the difficulty of producing a 'quality' requirements specification. We now consider three major influences on the achievement of such quality: form of representation, automated specification tools, and requirements validation.

Representation

We communicate with each other through the use of natural language. The component parts of such language – as all good literature reveals – provide the writer with a breadth of meaning. Unfortunately, breadth of meaning and ambiguity are very closely related and it is for this reason that natural language is not at all a satisfactory notation in which to present a specification of requirements. Explicit statements, individual identifications, completeness – all are made that much harder to achieve with natural language.

The following example, based on one given by Cohen (1982), is a useful illustration of both problem and possible solution.

Would the statement, 'write a program that calculates square roots' constitute an acceptable specification of requirements? If the answer is no (and it should be) then how do we move forward? Essentially by asking questions and using the answers to improve the specification:

Q: What is a square root?
A: That number which, when multiplied by itself, yields the input value.

Q: What kind of numbers are we dealing with: positive/negative, real/integer ...?
A: Positive real numbers.

At this point, the glimmerings of a formal specification begin to emerge:

SQRT: $R \rightarrow R$ [defines a partial function on real numbers only]

pre-SQRT(r) = $r \geqslant 0$ [further limited to positive numbers]

post-SQRT(r1,r2) = r1 = r2$\star$r2   [input/output relation]

Q: What if the answer can't be calculated exactly?
A: An adequate approximation will do.

Q: Define adequate!
A: When you multiply the result by itself, it should differ from the input by less than some small, positive non-zero value.

The specification is revised:

SQRT: R × R → R [to reflect that there are now two input parameters]

pre-SQRT(r,e) = r⩾0 and e>0 [the second being the 'error']

post-SQRT(r1,e,r2) = (r1−e) ⩽ (r2⋆r2) ⩽ (r1+e) [revised input/ output relation]

In this way the specification would be successively developed, with each question and its answer leading towards a more 'formal', less ambiguous, description of the user requirements.

The above (which uses a notation similar to that of Jones (1980) is but one example of formality − diagrams, tables, state charts and many others have been applied. All have the disadvantage, of course, of making the specification progressively less readable to the untrained eye.

In terms of quality control, this is not unimportant. Although the primary consideration has to be precision − in order that there be no doubts in the mind of the software designer about what the specification means − errors of understanding can easily creep in if the user cannot read the requirements document for his or her own system.

Thus a composite approach is normally taken, which incorporates both formal and informal methods of representation. A current example of this approach which is attracting a sizeable (but, hopefully, not cult) following is that of the specification language Z (Sufrin 1981), in which the document is written in a combination of formal set theory notation and informal English text.

Current thinking (partly determined by existing constraints due to a lack of tools − see Section 6.3 below) is that formal methods should certainly be used at the initial specification stage. In this way the costs associated with the additional time spent are outweighed by the savings which accrue from the enhanced capability for error detection at the earliest point in the development cycle.

Given that an (almost) error-free specification results, the level of formality during the design and implementation phases would be expected to reduce since, unless a suitably wide range of tools is available, the costs would probably outweigh the benefits.

Validation

Given the importance that we have emphasised should be attached to the requirements specification, it would indeed be incongruous not to stress with equal vigour the necessity for such specifications to undergo various levels of validation.

Like all aspects of the software development cycle this would be an iterative process, in this case around two separate aspects:

- production of the specification by an analyst
- confirmation, with the customer, that the specification accords with what the customer actually wants

Having produced a first attempt at a (formal) specification, the analyst will initially be concerned with asking, in effect, 'have I produced a valid specification of some system?' (Ignoring, to a great extent, whether or not it is exactly what the customer wants.) In this respect the analyst must check:

Consistency:

- of notation
- of interpretation of the operating environment
- of user/system interfaces

Completeness:

- all features are described
- all error conditions have been identified
- all system actions (normal and error-handling) have been specified

Having covered this ground, the requirements specification has to be presented to the customer for validation at the user level. If the analyst has used a formal method of specification, then some interpretation will certainly be necessary. This problem may not completely disappear, however, even with the specification incorporating a natural language component; it is almost inevitable that the specification will still include a certain amount of jargon, making it more difficult for the customer (and, if the truth be stated, the analyst) to imagine how the system will look in practice.

Consequently, the most beneficial form of validation at this level will be that of 'animating' the specification. The objective here is to show the customer, by means of a computer demonstration/simulation of some sort, precisely what has been defined. It is at this point that things start to become a little circular. Computer demonstrations imply implementation of the system that the requirements specification is concerned with defining before it can be implemented! In practice, therefore, animation basically requires the development of a prototype system showing, at the very least, the user interface elements proposed. This should cover most of the contentious points. Ultimately, of course, one must be looking forward to the development of formal methods of notation that can be executed in the way that a computer program is executed.

6.3 Software design

Principles

In the next phase of the life cycle, the 'what' of a requirements specification is used to produce the 'how' – the implementation details – of a software design.

This software system design, or architecture, is crucial to the successful development of a software system. Like a good route map, a good design will ensure that, if followed carefully, the project will progress successfully to its eventual destination. A bad design, however, will make the journey lengthy and frustrating and, conceivably, might even result in the destination not being reached at all.

In simple terms the design of the software architecture, like the design of a building, results in a 'paper' definition of what the structure will look like when complete. In the case of a building, the design is concerned with rooms, passageways and pipework. With software the design will cover analogous software entities: the components of the software system, the interfaces between those components and the nature of their interactions.

The importance attached to the production of good-quality software design may be indicated by the uses to which it is put.

- It is the first step taken by the developer which attempts to create a software system to satisfy the requirements. In this respect, therefore, design is a second-level form of validation – confirmation that it is indeed possible for the requirements to be implemented.
- The design will thus be the starting point for developing any prototype systems, either for the purposes of demonstration (in addition to, or possibly as part of, the 'animation' system described above) or for subsequent refinement of the system design itself.
- The design is also the basis for planning the remainder of the software development. The architecture will not only identify all software components which have to be produced with details of external and internal interfaces and interactions, but will also indicate the size and complexity of each of these components.

- Once this level of implementation detail has been defined, it is perfectly possible to begin to devise test specifications. Or, to put it another way, the design specifies what it is that has to be tested. The software design, therefore, almost as a by-product, forms the basis of test design.
- From the software (and test) designs it is possible to gauge much more accurately the level of implementation effort needed and, thereby, the duration of the project development. Design therefore also provides a basis for phasing implementation and delivery.

Design has to be recognised for what it is: a creative activity. It is inevitable that different designers will produce different software solutions to the same implementation problem.

So far as quality considerations are concerned this is not a cause for concern. Differences in the design process itself, however, are another matter. A software designer must accept that a uniformity of approach will be needed – a methodology.

Methodologies

Methodologies exist to provide the designer with an operational framework, although it has to be said that there are still a number of reactionaries who regard the word 'methodology' as being almost synonymous with 'straitjacket'. This is unfortunate; the correct use of a design methodology has too many implications for software quality to be ignored. It should:

- assist in the essential activities of design: abstraction, decomposition, elaboration and decision-making
- increase the visibility of the software design (i.e. its relationship to the requirements specification
- serve to identify review and testing points
- provide a clear division of design from implementation
- encourage phased development of the software
- ensure compatibility between designs produced by different designers
- help to minimise the problems of interpretation and future maintenance

(Strictly speaking, methodologies are by no means limited to the design aspects of the life cycle. However, since all of them, whatever their emphasis, are used with the design phase, it does not seem unreasonable to prefer to focus on them in a discussion on software design.)

The characteristics of a methodology are many and various; Jackson (1982) refers to something like eighty or more miscellaneous criteria that could be applied. Grouping them into five major categories, Jackson gives a useful checklist for use when considering a software development methodology. Some questions which might be asked about the design capability are as follows:

Notation (i.e. recording of information)

- what sort of notation does the methodology have?
- is it formal or informal?
- does it have any theoretical basis?
- does it represent any semantic aspects?
- how does it decompose problems (function-oriented or data-oriented)?
- is the notation easy to understand?
- can it be used for system documentation?

Procedure (i.e. step-by-step instructions for use)

- does the methodology have a systematic 'algorithmic' procedure for its use?
- does it promote a top-down or bottom-up strategy, or both?
- does it suggest certain solutions and inhibit others?
- would different practitioners reach similar solutions?
- does it effectively separate development concerns?

Checking

- what checks can be made within an output from a life cycle phase?
- what checks can be made between phases? (requirements versus design, say)
- does it provide for, or impose, audits and/or reviews?
- does it support the signing-off of phases?
- is it good for 'animation'?

(Actual details of any particular methodology are beyond the scope of this book; interested readers are referred to DTI(1985) as a good starting point, in particular Chapter 5 which provides an analysis of prevailing methods and tools.)

Widening the issue somewhat, it should be expected that more than one methodology will be be employed during the whole development life cycle from requirements specification through to maintenance. Certainly this is the case at present since, with the exception of CADES, no single development method attempts to address the whole range of activities. Most concentrate on specific areas. For example, methods such as CORE, SADT, SREM and other 'structured systems analysis' types focus primarily on requirements analysis; the more formally-based techniques such as HOS and VDM on the derivation of functionally correct designs; MASCOT on low-level design.

Current thinking suggests that this is not unreasonable, since it is expected that the enormously wide variety of applications to be found in industry and commerce would require correspondingly diverse methods of producing solutions. In many ways this appears analogous to the development of programming languages in which special-purpose languages have managed to survive (and even flourish) in the face of repeated attempts to replace them with megalanguages supposedly capable of universal application. Whether the latest attempt (Ada) will finally ring the death knell for special-purpose languages remains to be seen.

Design verification

To quote Denvir (1980), 'It is the responsibility of designers to state and record their reasons for believing their designs to be correct.' This is the essence of design verification – showing to an acceptable level of confidence that what has been produced is consistent with the requirements as specified.

In a fully formal approach, such verification would comprise a formal proof of correctness as each and every layer of detail was added. The literature is not short of examples; nowhere near so short as the examples themselves. Therein lies the rub: a formal verification of a design, as Somerville (1985) points out, will involve more effort than writing and subsequently proving the implementation in terms of a computer program. In terms which are readily understood by hard-nosed business people, formal methods at this level are not yet cost effective.

A more practical approach is what is known as a 'rigorous', as opposed to a formal, verification. That is, to work within a formal framework but to use informal arguments. Currently this approach is prevailing for three reasons:

- it requires less specialism on the part of the designer, with the reduced emphasis on formal notation in favour of language which is less 'obscure'
- the method of verification thereby lends itself more fully to the proven benefits of the design review, described in detail in Chapter 5. A number of different viewpoints may thus play a part in the verification process
- even rigorous verification is time consuming. The time can be cut down by the use of automated methods; most of those which are currently available support 'informal' rather than 'formal' methodologies

This last point is important and relates to the specification of requirements using a formal method also. Until such time as tools are widely available to support such techniques, their use is not likely to be as widespread as the problems demand that it should.

6.4 Tools

The quality benefits which one would expect to derive from the use of software development tools can perhaps be illustrated by a non-software example. Imagine a plumber who needs to saw a piece of pipe in half. He (she) might bend it repeatedly until it breaks; attack it with a karate chop; or use a cutting tool. Only the latter method gives us any level of confidence concerning the likely accuracy of the outcome.

A summary of the ways in which software requirements specification and design can be supported by automated methods is as follows:

Represent the design
Make it possible, by a variety of means (such as graphical displays, windowing, etc. and input devices such as light pens, mice, etc.) to quickly and easily build up the representation of the design in the way in which it is to be presented in the final design documentation.

Assist the design process
This can be done by providing mechanisms for the creative aspects of design, the capability to try things out, assessing the affects of changes, making automatic comparisons with earlier design attempts.

Give visibility to all aspects of the design
Enable direct links to be established and monitored in relation to the design currently in progress and that from which it is being derived. An obvious example would be visibility of requirements through to the different levels of software design.

Record, and recall, the design
There are two aspects here. The first is the obvious one of providing some mechanism for a machine-recordable (and, *ergo*, a machine-readable) design. The second, and complementary, aspect is that of extending the feature to provide what amounts to a design library mechanism. In this way (proven) designs may be accessed for reference or, in what amounts to an attempt to prevent the repeated invention of the wheel, for use.

Analyse and check the design for accuracy and consistency
With automatic means of validation and verification as outlined above.

Manage the complexity of the task
In other words, tools for administration must be available. Areas such as version control, documentation, etc. would be handled here.

The development of the programming language Ada has been heralded as something of a breakthrough in this respect. Here, not only has a new programming language been specified, but also an Ada Programming Support Environment (APSE) as well.

McDermid and Ripken (1984), following on from Buxton (1980), outline a minimal APSE (MAPSE): '(it) must contain the basic development support tools (compiler, editor, debugger ..), and most importantly, it must provide a database management system with a schema definition mechanism, and a database traversal and navigation mechanism based on a query language.'

From this base position it is assumed that an APSE might develop in three stages:

Stage 1: Clerical support APSE

- structural editors
- syntactic analysers
- report generators

Stage 2: Verification, validation and management support APSE

- semantic checkers
- browsing facility
- graphical editor
- configuration management facilities
- PERT/critical path analyser
- project guide manipulation tool
- communication path definition tool
- progress monitoring and indication tools
- graphical display tool
- various language-specific (Ada) testing tools

Stage 3: Transformation support APSE

- transformation drivers to generate life cycle representations for a new representation level
- modelling and simulation tools
- rapid implementation and prototyping tools

- symbolic execution
- program prover
- estimation and statistical analysis tools
- work breakdown tool
- resource allocation aid

Many of these features exist, of course, in current methodologies and their associated tools; what is different in this respect is that APSE proposals aim at a coherent tool-set to cover each and every phase of the development life cycle.

Estimates range between 80 and 160 man-years of effort to produce such an environment – and even that assumes the starting condition of an available MAPSE! Quality software will be achieved only at a price.

7 Code

It is a commonly held, but fallacious, view that quality control on program code means the activity of testing. Testing, as will be seen in Chapter 8, is only one aspect of code quality control, albeit a major one.

The reason for this is that testing, by its very nature, seeks to uncover errors; a lack of quality, if you like. But the easiest way of dealing with coding faults is to avoid their creeping in to begin with. In this chapter, therefore, we examine factors which can influence the quality of program code at the outset.

7.1 Programming languages

Choice of programming language

Coding effectively begins with the choice of a programming language in which to implement the design. The approach is obvious. A multiplicity of languages exist; the problem is to select, from the many hundreds in existence, that which is best suited to the application. (Although a gross over-simplification, the 'best-suited' language is deemed to be that which enables the final program code to reflect most consistently the program design; in this way quality control is clearly made easier.) This is fine in theory, but impossible to carry out in practice.

To begin with, the design itself will influence matters. The reason for this is that, even though a design is expected to be language-independent, it will necessarily affect the choice of language both by its assumption that the design is capable of realisation in whatever programming language is used and, to a lesser extent, by the design methodology employed. Shaw *et al.* (1981) gives a number of 'core' criteria by which languages can be judged, such as lexical and syntactic issues, data and data structure issues, and control structure issues. Such design influence though, being more to do with the structures and facilities offered by the language in general rather than language specifics, would still leave an enormous number of languages to choose from.

In practice, however, even at best a free choice is only ever available from a very short list. At worst, the language will have been determined before design has even started. Some of the reasons for this are:

(a) No ideal language exists. In such a case then the alternatives are to invest in designing a new, ideal, language and writing a translator for it, or to make the most of a language that is less than ideal. The former choice can be practical for very large projects: the language C aided and abetted the development of the UNIX operating system, for instance. For smaller projects this is not likely to be an option.

(b) A translator for the chosen programming language may not be available for the hardware configuration, and its acquisition may be too expensive to consider.

(c) Existing programming staff may not be fluent in the ideal language, and the problem of retraining may be too massive.

(d) Previous projects may have been written in a different language. Apart from the fact that experience will thus be available in the use of this other language, it could be a deciding factor if the previous projects are in any way related to the project under discussion. (Note that this argument is, of course, self-perpetuating for the language chosen.)

(e) The user may stipulate that a particular programming language is to be used, or chosen from a short list. This applies to Ministry of Defence contracts, for instance, which stipulate Ada as the language to be used. Unless the customer can be persuaded to accept an alternative, then a choice just does not exist at all.

Purely in terms of quality control requirements, the first three criteria above should not come into play; in terms of economics, however, they always will. For the other criteria the position is less simple. Quality control embraces not just development but maintenance also; making the function easier by selecting the ideal language for every individual project may make life much harder *in toto*.

Types of programming language

The nature of the ideal language will vary dramatically from one project to another. The main categories of programming language are considered below, both in terms of their likelihood of being selected and of the subsequent quality control problems that such a selection would provoke.

Second-generation (assembly) languages

Assembly languages operate in terms of machine-level detail. Programs written in assembler therefore take much longer to write and debug; the language is almost wholly unstructured, leading to code which disguises design detail so completely that it is virtually impossible to identify the context for any group of program statements; by virtue of their close relationship with the machine architecture, they open up new vistas for weird and wonderful programming errors. Quality control and assembly language programming pull in opposite directions.

Only one valid reason exists for the use of assembly language and that is enhanced performance. Compiler-generated machine code, even optimised, may not be efficient enough to meet critical execution timings. In such cases the use of assembly language should be a matter of re-coding that part of a high-level language system which needs speeding up. In this way a design/high-level program/assembler-level trio provide the tractability that quality control needs.

Third-generation (or high-level) languages

Although the vast proportion of languages will fall into this category, only a few will realistically be contenders for most projects.

Amongst these, for scientific and commercial applications respectively, will inevitably be FORTRAN and COBOL. Pressman (1982) has called these languages (along with BASIC and ALGOL) 'foundation languages'. The term is revealing. Both have been repeatedly criticised over their 25+ years of life, but yet remain viable options for software implementations. The reasons are salutary and of particular relevance to quality control. Both languages have evolved, their features and facilities developing to meet new demands, but 'upwards-compatibility' has remained: a program written in original FORTRAN/COBOL, for instance, will still be valid under the most recent versions. Quality control has been aided by the ability thus given for verified software to be re-used. Also, both languages have been the subject of defined standards, each version arriving in tandem with the new standard; portability – another quality control benefit – has thus been enhanced.

Thus, in spite of the fact that both languages exhibit a lack of structure, weak data typing, general incomprehensibility – all of which make quality control of new software developments in these languages that much harder – FORTRAN and COBOL will remain prime candidates for selection when the new software is building on some that is old and reliable. Much the same could be said for PL/1 and IBM-based systems.

What is equally salutary is why the 'block-structured' alternatives in the third-generation arena did not attain popularity. Essentially, this was due to their being less easy to use in an era in which design activity came a poor second to programming. Thus ALGOL-60 lost out to FORTRAN and COBOL, and Pascal was dismissed as an 'academic' language suitable for teaching principles but of little use in practice. The stipulation that, in the UK, Ministry of Defence contracts be implemented in CORAL 66 was one of the few successes – and only then when not ignored.

This situation has changed. Languages which enforce control and data structuring are now accepted for their value in assisting the process of quality control. The realisation that language structures, by facilitating program code which flows directly from design structures, automatically generate the crucial quality control factor of tractability, is a prime example. This is reflected in the major programming language development effort in our time; although calling it a third-generation language is to stretch a definition somewhat, the language Ada, developed under the direction of the US Department of Defense as their language for the future, is the apotheosis of a structured language. It is now mandatory for all US and UK defence projects; its impact in the wider world of industry remains to be seen.

The more fanatical proponents of Ada see it eventually replacing all other languages. Time will tell. Underneath the hype Ada is still an, albeit very powerful, third-generation language. To assume dominance Ada will need to prove itself capable of meeting the needs of a vast range of applications currently implemented in 'special-purpose' languages: systems development (BCPL, C), string handling (SNOBOL), report generation (RPG), simulation (SIMULA), list processing and artificial intelligence (LISP and PROLOG) are but a few.

Fourth-generation languages
The perceived disadvantage of the third-generation languages is that they are 'technical' in nature; in other words, application programs need to be written by a programming specialist. The principle behind fourth-generation languages (4GLs) is that they enable programs to be developed by non-specialists, thereby speeding applications development.

4GLs operate more in terms of structures (both code and data) than in executable steps. In essence, such languages provide fixed coding frameworks to which the 'programmer' adds detail. By removing the third-generation mechanics of constructing these frameworks each and every time they are needed, the 4GL theoretically enables program development to be carried out nearer to the 'user' level. In practice, however, much the same programming skills are required to use 4GLs well. Also, recourse often has to be made to a third-generation (most typically, COBOL) language to code areas which the 4GL cannot handle satisfactorily. The third-generation programmer lives on.

But although 4GLs (which proliferate no less rapidly than their third-generation predecessors) may not have attained their original objective, they have nevertheless precipitated advances from the quality viewpoint. Use of a 4GL enforces structured programming. Furthermore, in the hands of a skilled practitioner, program development in a 4GL is made significantly faster; this has encouraged the use of prototyping – the development of early 'throw-away' versions of a software system – enabling the production of requirements specifications which are not beset by misunderstandings between user and developer.

Perhaps most significantly, the 4GL approach has encouraged the use of software tools. Report generators, application generators, database manipulation languages, screen formatters: these and other tools have emerged as essential companions to the programming language. Each enforces quality by automating error-prone tasks. The project support environment, which we consider further in Section 7.2 below, is the result.

Mixed-language programming

Whilst the world waits for the Ada language and its associated development tools to assume total dominance, a short-term – and probably more likely – development is an increased use of mixed-language programming.

The concept is attractive in terms of potential for quality control. A system design has its various parts implemented not in one single language which although generally suitable might be quite unsuitable for some parts, but in a combination of languages with each design section coded in the language best suited to the task. The use of 4GLs and COBOL in mixed quantities is an example of the approach, as is the mixed use of high-level language and assembly language coding with real-time applications. Other possibilities in the future might be the implementation of 'intelligent' real-time systems through a combination of, say, Ada and PROLOG. Quality control can only be made easier by an approach such as this which produces code which most accurately reflects design.

Mixed-language programming can play a useful part in maintenance also. Enhancements to existing software written in a less-than-ideal language need not slavishly be written in that same language. A more modern, and more suitable, language can be employed for the new code. This has been quite successfully achieved with the admixture of 4GLs and COBOL, for instance.

The stumbling block, inevitably, is that different language translation systems may not support mixed-language programming. It is necessary that a common intermediate form be produced at some stage to enable 'mixture' to take place, a point which will now be considered as one of the many needs catered for by program development tools.

7.2 Program development tools

Automation of the steps involved in program coding enables those steps to be carried out quickly, accurately and consistently. The first of these, speed, was recognised first: hand-production of machine code provoked the development of assemblers to accelerate the process. Cutting development time has been the catalyst for software tools production ever since. Only comparatively recently, however, has the realisation dawned that a set of good software development tools also enables the quality requirements of accuracy and consistency.

In simple terms, program development involves:

- preparation of an item of program source code
- translation of this code into a machine-level form
- linking of the machine code with other, similar items to form a program that can be executed
- verification of that program's run-time performance
- amendment of the original source program so as to remove errors and effect a return to the preparation step

These steps are now considered as regards tools to ease the task. Verification is important enough to warrant its own chapter and will not be covered explicitly. Preparation is a subset of the final amendment step of course (since the latter necessarily involves the preparation of source code) and the two will be considered together.

Editors

On the reasonable assumption that a source program is to be held in a disc file, there are requirements to create that file in the first place and, subsequently, to alter its contents. An interactive tool, an editor, is used for this purpose. In general terms, editors are either wholly line-based or wholly screen-based, or some combination of the two.

Line-based editing is an anachronism, dating back to the teletype days before screens replaced paper. The system commands enable a user to work through his or her file line by line, with only the 'current line' being available for alteration at one time. A display of this line, which often has to be requested, is necessary for the user to confirm that the source file is being edited in the correct place. Not surprisingly, with a system which hides so much information by design, use of a line editor can often cause the introduction of more errors than it removes.

Screen editing systems present a full screen of text at a time, and the user locates an editing position by moving a cursor around the screen. In this way edits are seen to be effected correctly; an obvious feature, but one still not implemented in a truly comprehensive manner on a number of major computer systems.

Context-sensitive editors take screen editing a stage further. They are language-oriented. Thus a COBOL program file would be modified using its related editor, a tool which incorporates not only editing capability but also features such as automatic structure generation for the language in question and diagnostic information for the user when statements are input which are syntactically incorrect.

Translators

Before a program can be run it has to be translated into a form suitable for execution. At the risk of an over simplification, there are two broad approaches to this task of translation: the source code can be interpreted or compiled.

An interpreter translates a source statement and executes it straight away. This applies to every statement, whether or not that statement has been met before – as it would be, for instance, in an iterative loop. Inevitably, therefore, interpretation results in execution times which are considerably longer than for compiled code. One of the problems with 4GL systems currently available is that many of them are interpreter-based. On the credit side, however, the ready availability of the source code enables an interpretive system to give a clear indication as to the type and location of execution errors when they occur. Combined with an integrated source code editor, an interpretive system can undoubtedly make software development that much easier and quicker.

Compilation, on the other hand, causes the complete transformation of a source text from an external to an internal form: program instructions are converted into their respective machine-executable statements, symbolic names are converted into machine addresses with associated memory blocks, and so on. By considering the whole source text as a single entity a compiler is able to resolve many complex error conditions – such as the scope of variables and illegal accesses, inappropriate nesting of loops and sub-programs, incomplete control constructs – at an earlier stage than an interpretive system.

Whichever approach is taken, effective error messages are vital. An error message should attempt to indicate two things: the type of error detected, and its whereabouts. Nothing is gained by unquestioning acceptance of a language translator which is inadequate in this respect.

The generally accepted principles of structured design mean that a complex system will be developed by breaking it into a number of smaller, less complex, subsystems, each of which can be independently compiled (another requirement of the compilation system) and validated before being combined with other subsystems. Working in this way it is easy for a change in any small part of the whole program to be effected quickly, by simply editing and recompiling the faulty module rather than the whole program.

Independent compilation also enables the construction of libraries of precompiled modules which can be incorporated into a program. Routines which are of use to a large number of programs are written and fully tested. They are then compiled, the object modules being stored in what is termed an object library file on disc; from here they can be added to a program without having to be compiled again. This approach is regularly employed with the 'run-time library' for a language system – in providing its input/ output routines, for instance. By holding the object code for these functions in a separate library file, portability is enhanced by enabling routines for the configuration in use to be added in a way that does not require changes to the source program.

The compiled code generated in this case will not, therefore, be machine code but some intermediate form. The assembly language of the target machine is one possibility. Though limiting portability this technique does enable the compiler output to be modified by hand at a later stage, if key areas need increased efficiency for performance reasons; it also assists the inclusion of assembly language sections in the high-level program.

Whatever the intermediate form, however, the need will exist for tools to integrate a number of such modules to form a complete software system – linkers.

Linkers

Linking (or link editing) involves the collecting together of object modules, either user-generated as the product of compilation or already available through a system object library, to form a single entity. The basic function of the linker is to resolve cross-references between the routines, e.g. calls by one routine of a procedure that is declared in another routine, with unsatisfied references being flagged as errors.

The process is command-driven, a list of files being specified for the linker to work on. Figure 7.1 illustrates the process.

A linker thus supports the modular approach to software development. It is worth pointing out at this stage, however, that from the quality control viewpoint the automation of module linking can be its own worst enemy. If the correct routines are integrated, then the linker provides a valuable service; if incorrect (most typically, not-the-latest-version) routines are specified, then problems are spawned which may not hatch out for quite some time.

Essentially, we are talking about an aspect of software configuration management. A linking mechanism, therefore, should comprise not just a tool which blindly cobbles together programs from individual routines but one that incorporate facilities for version control.

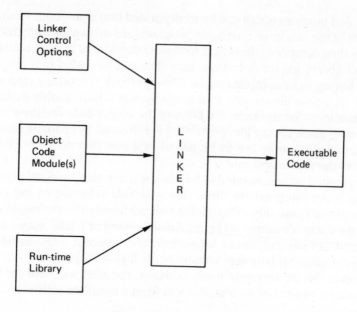

Figure 7.1. The linking process

Integrated program support environments

The foregoing has dealt with fundamental software development tools as independent items; and that, in many instances, is how they exist – as utility programs called into action one at a time.

An integrated environment seeks to provide a unified toolkit rather than a collection of odd items. Integration exists at three levels:

- function: for instance, automatic progression through the stages of compilation, linkage and execution
- data: in order that different tools may share data entities: typically a support tool will 'centre' on a database
- interface: a common (e.g. menu-driven) interface for the user so as to offer a consistent method of accessing the tools

In this way the development process is accelerated. Moreover, the support environment can be extended to encompass (as was mentioned in Chapter 6, and will be mentioned again in Chapter 8) other aspects of the development life cycle:

- prototyping
- formal specification
- structural and detailed design
- requirements capture

- requirements specification
- environment management
- tool integration
- standard system tools
- code and unit test
- validation, verification and test

This list is being extended still further as IPSE environments develop in which the P stands for 'project' rather than 'programming'. Additions in this respect will handle configuration management, project management, quality assurance, document handling and office automation. Finally, one further requirement to cater for future and/or local special needs is the capability to embrace user-defined tools, or tools ported from other IPSEs.

In quality control terms the benefits are clear: automation of the life cycle, provision of good, verified development tools – all assist in the production of a development environment which minimises the opportunities for the introduction of 'man-made' errors. Furthermore, the actual 'man-made' parts can be reduced further – a database of design representations facilitates the automatic production of code, for instance.

At present, however, this is something of a counsel of perfection. The IPSE is evolving, just as programming languages have evolved; evaluation is no less necessary with the former, therefore, than with the latter. As major IPSE evaluation criteria Higgs (1987) cites the following:

- flexibility: to avoid being locked into particular methodologies, project management structures and data management systems
- tool integration: to ensure a wide choice and the ability to adapt the system
- life cycle coverage: to enable integration of tools to cover all activities in the software life cycle
- functionality: to do what the user requires
- performance: and at an acceptable speed
- project management aids: to enable management to estimate, plan and control all tasks and the deployment of staff
- interfaces: to provide a common method of accessing tools

7.3 Defensive programming techniques

Programming languages and development tools support quality control by facilitating a good, accurate transition from design to code. What they are unable to influence, however, is the logical correctness of that design or that code.

In one respect that falls upon the testing phase, which we look at in the next chapter. But in an important respect, however, it is also a matter for the programmer at the coding stage. A well-written program will not only be free of logical errors but will also contain sequences that prevent run-time errors (whether caused by user and/or environment) from occurring or, at least, from spreading and turning into something serious.

Some languages will support defensive programming, as such prevention is termed, better than others; none will be able to force a programmer to program defensively in the first place. Defensive programming is more a state of mind than a technique or a methodology, a desire to cover every eventuality inculcated by the adoption of good quality control practices. The following representative examples of defensive programming would, if present, be a positive indication that development had been conducted by such a mind.

Programming for error containment

Data initialisation
On some computer configurations the first appearance of a data object can be assumed to have an initial value – zero, typically. Defensive programming would explicitly initialise the content of all such variables as part of the program code. Unless this is done the program could fail in a random fashion – on re-entry to the code with the variable non-zero, for instance.

The same problem applies to the initial setting of values for larger data structures such as arrays. Here, the action will often involve the reading of data from a file – a process difficult to check visually.

Constants are data objects which do not change their value during the execution of a program. Building constants, rather than their numeric values, into the program code lessens the chances of error if that value is ever changed; not so doing necessitates alterations to every point in the program at which the value is used.

There should be sensible assignment of variable types to the values they represent. A blanket use of real variables, for instance, will at some stage involve a comparison of two reals which may work in theory (and be supported by run-time output) but fail in practice. Also, in terms of performance, use of integer variables (and boolean variables, which amount to the same thing) will increase processing speeds. Computers take less time to carry out integer arithmetic than real arithmetic, and execution times can be halved through the use of integer variables rather than real variables.

Data subranges

Every data value will have a range of permitted values. The use of a language's subrange feature (assuming it exists) is defensive programming made easy. By declaring in a subrange the expected values for a variable, an automatic checking mechanism will be invoked if that range is exceeded.

A similar technique should be employed with arrays, since the dimension of an array is effectively a subrange itself (of the index to access the array). Array bound checking alone, i.e. detecting the point at which an attempt is made to access the array with an illegal subscript, is not good enough. What the programmer wants to know is where the illegal subscript was generated, and that may be some distance away – especially if the index is being passed as a parameter to a procedure which manipulates the array. Use of a subrange for both the index and the array bound will cover all eventualities.

Note, however, that range checking such as this incurs a price in terms of performance since additional system code has to be obeyed at run-time. Lose the overhead, which is usually an option, and the facility is lost too.

Data input

All input data should be checked for validity before being passed on to the rest of the program for processing. Although much of this checking can be carried out by the use of subrange facilities if they exist, there will necessarily be a number of other things that can go wrong.

Another potential problem is loss of data: that is, data values not actually reaching the program at all. This fault is readily apparent if the program is being run interactively, but not so if input is being taken from backing store. There, loss of one data item can mean that a whole series of variables end up with the wrong values with, at worst, incorrect results being generated. Defensive programming requires that input values should not only be valid, but be seen to be valid: when in doubt, print it out.

Again a price has to be paid for run-time quality. It is possible that for complex data entry the program statements for validation can quite easily amount to a significant proportion of the overall code.

Exception handling

A major problem area is that of the system error, a fault condition detected either by the computer operating system or the language system's run-time routines. In such cases only two choices are available. The first is to accept that the program will be regarded by the operating system as being beyond help, and summarily abandoned with an error message likely to mean very little to the user.

The second, which requires much more effort, is to implement an 'exception handling' routine which will take command of the situation and try to recover from it. The effort involved here is considerable, since all possible eventualities have to be catered for. Unfortunately, even if this course is followed (which, ideally, it should be), the programming language is likely to be found wanting: the one exception is Ada.

Exception handling is a minefield. For instance, even if a routine has been written, and can be entered automatically, what happens after the routine has been executed? Is it possible to recover the situation and continue with the program run? If so, at what point? Even a nice 'clean' solution such as returning to the menu presentation part of the main program is likely to leave an untidy position behind in terms of incomplete procedure calls. Somerville (1985) raises the questions that need to be borne in mind when assessing programming language design in this area; these can equally well be turned into quality control questions regarding a program's design:

- Are exceptions declared? They should be.
- Where are exception handlers placed in the program? Location and easy identification is desired.
- Are the exception handlers a distinct program structure, or are exceptions handled using existing structures such as procedures? Either may be satisfactory so long as the structure does the job.
- How are exceptions signalled and transmitted from one program unit to another? Some mechanism is needed to avoid a multiplicity of testing.
- Are exceptions and exception handlers subject to the normal scope and extent rules of the language? Ideally they should be, but this may just not be possible if error recovery is to be effected; if scope rules are to be flouted, however, it should be done with full regard to the ramifications.
- Do exception handlers cause control to be returned to the point where the exception occurred after the exception has been dealt with? If not, where? The lack of a rigid formula is excusable, but a lack of consistency is not.

Developments in the language Ada appear to have made significant strides in the direction of adequate structures for exception handling; the reader is referred to Barnes (1984), or any of the many other texts on Ada, for further information.

7.4 Standards

The question of standards

As we have pointed out above, a major stumbling block to effective quality control is the sheer multiplicity of programming languages and development tools, both in their definition and in the conventions and procedures which govern their use. Incompatibilities between different versions of the same programming language, compilers which inhibit the development of mixed-language programs through production of different intermediate code structures, software tools and databases which cannot be ported from one system to another; all are examples of a lack of standardisation.

It is the adoption of a 'standard' – agreed and shared rules of system design and behaviour – that enables control to be exercised effectively.

Ideally the standard will be the product of careful thought, evaluation and refinement. This process, however, demands time before the product – a programming language or whatever – is brought into use. The development of Ada is such an instance, and an example of the growing maturity of the software industry. Evidence that this time has not been available during the software industry's mushroom growth is the *de facto* standard: a standard which is adopted, not because it is necessarily the best (and the operating systems MS-DOS and UNIX are classic examples in this respect), but because it is widely used. This practice is continuing, as the world-wide acceptance of the IBM-PC standard shows.

Good or bad, however, it might be argued that any standard is better than no standard at all. This is an argument that has some merit, but only if the standard is not open to varying interpretation – in which case it becomes a guideline and nothing more – and the standard is usable. Ould and Thewlis (1987) summarise the criteria for a standard's usability:

- it must explain what the ends are, what the standard aims to achieve: it must explain its *raison d'être* to help the developer determine whether or not it is appropriate to a given situation
- it must be testable, to determine whether or not it has been followed in a particular case
- it must be appropriate to both to the development approach and method in use
- it must be appropriate to the development tools in use
- it should prescribe activities and products that are clerical in nature, and prescribe qualititative criteria for activities and products that are not simply clerical

Software development standards can be broadly classified under one of two headings:

- a process standard such as AQAP-13, which details the procedures to be followed for a software development project: how it is to be tackled, the steps to be followed, baselines to be established, reviews to be undertaken, and so on.
- a product standard such as the language implementation (compiler) in which the software is to be written, or the development tools to be employed.

The content of procedural standards, such as BS5750, DEFSTAN 00-16 and AQAP-13, has already been considered. Taking programming languages and development tools as examples, we now look at the general approach to product standards.

Programming language standards

A prime requirement for a high-level language system is that it should be machine independent. That is, a FORTRAN program written and developed using a compiler on one machine should successfully compile under a FORTRAN compiler running on another machine. Unfortunately, this eminently sensible approach is still the exception rather than the rule, which means that the 'porting' of a program from one machine to another is possible only at the expense of much error-prone re-coding. The reason is that compilers produced by computer manufacturers can be quite different, even though they are based on the same high-level language. Nobody benefits from this stupidity except the computer/compiler manufacturers, with users being tied to their particular products because of the volume of extra work needed to move elsewhere.

Clearly, language standards are essential, and have been for many years. From the Algol 60 Report, through to the latest Ada document, definitive statements have been produced on what constitutes a legal program in that language. Problems occur when these definitions are seen as the starting point, rather than finishing point, for language implementations with individual implementors adding to or deleting from this definition. The existence of a language standard, in stating that such-and-such a definition of a high-level language is to be regarded as the standard for compilers for that language, solves nothing in itself of course. Manufacturers are still at liberty to do as they will but, with a standard in existence, they are at least forced to define the ways in which their compiler implementations diverge from the accepted standard.

Language standards also enable compilers to be validated – that is, confirmed by some independent organisation to conform to the standard for that language. This provides a level of customer power, enabling a user to stipulate, as one of the non-functional requirements for software to be produced on his behalf, that software be written in a language for which the compiler has been validated. In this way users can at least assure compatibility between different software products produced on their behalf.

Typically, a compiler validation will result in a report which sets out the observed results from a series of tests designed to demonstrate that compiler's adherence, or lack of it, to the language standard. For instance, the National Computing Centre validation for COBOL compilers involves 300 programs, each of which comprise several individual tests. Successfully validated products will be certificated and added to a list of compilers which have current validation certificates; a sensible customer will ask for software to be compiled using one of the entries on such a list.

Development tools standards

Many of the same arguments can be applied to standards for development tools such as file editors, debugging and tracing systems and so on, but perhaps with less force. To take the file editor as a simple example, its development has been technology-driven; rigid adherence to a standard more suited to a teletype than a workstation would clearly have been a nonsense. In addition, development tools might rightly be claimed to be 'proprietary products', their capabilities being what gives one manufacturer's system the edge over another.

This is reflected in current thinking on the subject of standards for software engineering tools. The emphasis is not on the tools themselves following a standard form (although one would not expect to see different tools within an IPSE manifesting a variety of forms) but on the standard adopted for the interfaces between those tools. Two major projects are working towards this objective, albeit from different directions.

CAIS (Common APSE Interface Set) is the working name of a project sponsored by the US Department of Defense, the aim of which is to develop a standard set of Ada Programming Support Environments interfaces (USDOD1986a) and a set of Requirements and Design Criteria for CAIS (USDOD1986b). The opening paragraph of the 'General Requirements' chapter of the CAIS document gives the flavour of what that project is about:

'The CAIS provides interfaces for data storage and retrieval, data transmission to and from external devices, and activation of processes and control of their execution. In order to achieve uniformity in the interfaces, a single model is used to describe consistently general data storage, devices and executing programs. This approach provides a single model for understanding the CAIS concepts; it provides a uniform understanding of and emphasis on data storage and program control; and it provides a consistent way of expressing interrelations both within and between data and executing programs.'

The Portable Common Tool Environment (PCTE), is a project to design, implement and evaluate a tool interface, initiated in 1983 as part of the European Strategic Programme for Research and development in Information Technologies (ESPRIT). The intention is that PCTE specifications will be observed by tool providers, so permitting any software tools to be freely moved between computers for which a PCTE implementation is available (see Figure 7.2).

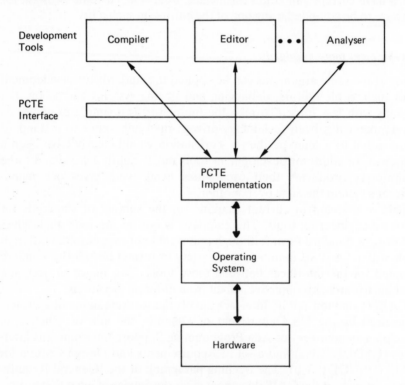

Figure 7.2. PCTE: Portable Common Tool Environment

There are four main parts to PCTE (ESPRIT 1986):

Basic mechanisms

- execution: how programs are executed, and how parameters are passed to a program
- communications: how a program accesses the contents of other objects

- inter-process communications: how synchronous processes communicate with each other

Object management system

- definition of object and link types, i.e. 'data items' with respect to their attributes and relationships with other objects
- rules for the creation and management of objects and links
- control over concurrent access to objects

User interface

- management of windows
- management of menus, etc.

Distribution

- management of workstations
- management of remote volumes, objects and processes

These initiatives seek to provide an environment for software development in which quality control mechanisms are enforced automatically: a standard method of enforcing standards. It is a worthy aim.

8   Test

8.1 Planning to test

The guiding principle of software quality control is, 'get it right first time'. For this reason the planning for a project will look forward to the day when an implemented version of the design is ready to be tested. It will aim to maximise the effectiveness of discovering errors by early and controlled production of test plans and test specifications.

A test plan is essentially a strategy document. It defines – for the project as a whole – testing philosophy, procedures to be followed, and test stages and their sequence. It will be complemented by a series of test specifications, which provide the detail for a particular test or series of tests.

In terms of quality control, these documents are crucial. If (or when) a project falls behind schedule, there is inevitably a great temptation to cut short the testing phases so as to meet the deadline. The existence of agreed test plans and specifications acts as a deterrent in this respect. Conversely, if test-trimming does occur, these documents provide a summary of what has been skimped.

Contents of the test plan

The test plan would be produced as early as possible in the project life cycle, and be updated whenever necessary in response to changes elsewhere in the development programme. It should address the three major areas mentioned below.

Test philosophy

A test philosophy states the approach to be taken in testing the product; as such, it should give a clear indication of the levels and degree of testing that are felt necessary, and upon which parts of the product. It will, for instance, decree at the outset that testing is required to be conducted at the module, sub-module and unit levels of the detailed design.

A further area of test philosophy deals with logistics. How is testing to be carried out in practice? For instance, will techniques such as simulation be allowed, and in what circumstances? It will describe how the testing activities are to be organised, when, and by whom, and cover all event-ualities in the conduct of a test, such as aborting and restarting a test run.

Similarly, the philosophy will determine what is to be the measure of 'testedness' – the criteria of success and failure for any test – and how it is to be determined in general.

Test stages and sequences

In very broad terms, three separate test stages are implied by the project life cycle:

- Module testing: 'independent' testing of sections of code. Since the terminology can become very suspect here, let us say that what we are talking about is the testing of the functionality of the module. Does it do what it is supposed to do? If the module is made up of a number of sub-modules and units then the same sort of test would be applied to each of these component sections.
- Integration testing: the testing of two or more modules operating together. Here the emphasis, assuming that module testing has done its job, is on proving the interactions between the modules: that they operate correctly as an integrated whole. Depending on the complexity of the system, integration tests may be conducted at a range of code levels.
- Acceptance testing: it works, but does it work properly? Testing for acceptance means using the software in a real situation (or an acceptably simulated one, e.g. for nuclear power station process control) in order to demonstrate that it meets the requirements specification, in terms of functionality and performance.

The test plan will relate these stages to the software design and to the requirements specification in order to identify the test stages for the project and, thereby, the objectives of the tests to be conducted at those stages.

It will also stipulate test sequences. Just what such a sequence should be for any particular system will require careful analysis. Much will depend upon the ways in which the various modules interrelate with each other; a well-planned ordering of the integration tests can exercise a wider range of possible events and also lessen the amounts of special-purpose test software that have to be produced. A carefully defined test sequence thus forms the basis for a production schedule.

Test procedures

General procedures for the conduct of tests are primarily concerned with:

- test results: procedures for documenting, summarising and reviewing the results of tests

- test failure (test success?): what to do when errors are discovered in the software being tested
- test changes: altering the agreed test specification/sequence for any reason
- test deliverables: the documents to be produced during the testing activities of the project. For example, Frewin and Hatton (1986) cite test logs, test incident reports, test summary reports, test input/output data (actual and intended) and test tools

Contents of a test specification

A test specification provides details for a specific test. Each test will be uniquely identified and documented so as to be available for later reference. Essentially, a test specification covers the what, why and how of testing.

What is to be tested
This could range from the test of a coded unit, or even a section of code, through to the integration test of a number of modules, up to the final acceptance testing of the final article.

Why it is to be tested
In other words, the objective of the test. Again the range is wide, from the proving of a particular algorithm through to the verification of a performance limitation. Whatever the case, the objective should relate to the appropriate part of the requirements specification.

How it is to be tested
This section comprises a number of parts:

- test data: items of data being used in the test
- test results: expected results using this data
- test records: how the results and findings are being recorded
- hardware: details of the configuration needed to support the test
- software: system and test software elements needed to support the test
- security: the level of security which must be provided for each of the above

This existence of a complete series of good specifications is evidence that the test plan has been read and put into practice. A complete set of test deliverables is evidence that the specifications have been read and put into practice. Taken *in toto*, these documents (and their associated computer-based data files) amount to a quality control audit trail that gives both a high level of confidence in the product and provides a sure information base for future maintenance.

8.2 Principles of testing

What, precisely, does any test set out to prove? In general terms, the aim of a test is to uncover errors. Paradoxically, perhaps, a successful test run is one which fails because an error has been detected.

The approach to the design of any particular test, therefore, will be dependent upon the nature of that which is being tested: its construction, its role in the overall scheme of things, and its interaction with other parts of the total software product. In the following sections we look at the major factors in software test design.

Top-down or bottom-up testing   *See Linda's Note*

The application of structured design techniques will have resulted in a hierarchical software design of modules, sub-modules and units. Top-down and bottom-up testing methods both reflect such a hierarchy.

Bottom-up testing involves the testing of lower-level units first, followed by the integration testing of combined units. In this way testing proceeds from the bottom of the design upwards.

Testing a unit in this way will require the additional development of a test harness, or driver, program. The driver effectively acts as part of the calling routine, exercising interfaces and sending and/or receiving test data and results. Figure 8.1 gives a 'snapshot' example of bottom-up implementation and testing for a collection of modules.

There are two main disadvantages of bottom-up testing. First, because testing of the complete system is, by definition, only carried out in the final stages, major design flaws do not show up until late in the day; inevitably the resolution of such errors will require some reworking (and thus retesting) of lower-level routines. Second, there is no visible, working system until the later stages of testing; pressures may build up which lead to testing being skimped in order to have something to 'show' the customer/ management.

Top-down testing does not simply work in the opposite direction; it necessarily dictates that testing and programming are dealt with side-by-side, with modules being tested immediately after they are written and before the programming of their subordinate modules. The maxim 'build a little, test a little' applies. Figure 8.2 reflects the top-down implementation and testing approach.

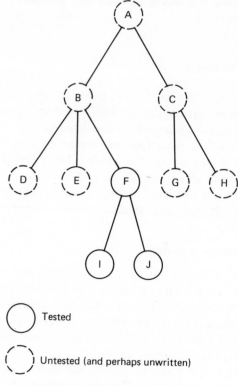

Figure 8.1. Bottom-up testing

Now on the face of it there appears to be a problem. How is it possible to test module B without having modules E and F that it calls? Similarly, how can module C claim to have been tested? The answer is that the 'absent' items in Figure 8.2 are actually present in the form of 'stubs': surrogate pieces of code which are replaced as and when the real thing is developed. Stubs have to be written too, of course, but the effort expended in their development need not be great; in their simplest form they need do little more than generate an 'I-was-here' message.

The major advantages of top-down testing overcome the disadvantages of bottom-up testing. Top-level design flaws are revealed quickly, since the higher levels of the hierarchy are tested first. For the most part, errors detected do not require other routines to be recoded. After any correction is made re-testing of all existing elements is carried out automatically. Also, a 'working' version is produced very quickly. Such implementations, although by definition 'top-level', are very useful in revealing flaws in requirements specifications.

The disadvantages of top-down testing, not unnaturally, tend to be the

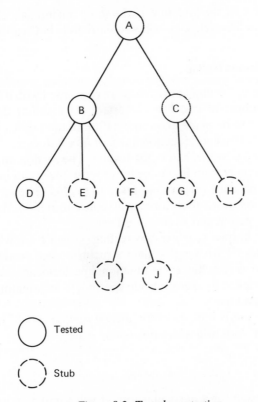

Figure 8.2. Top-down testing

advantages of the bottom-up approach. A software implementation will often have a few modules at a low level in its design hierarchy which are 'critical' for some reason – because they relate to performance or a key algorithm, for instance. Using a strict top-down approach, difficulties with critical modules would be discovered only towards the end of testing; this would obviously not be so with the bottom-up approach. Low-level modules are also quite often concerned with input/output. In bottom-up development and testing, these modules will quickly be available; top-down testing might well require widespread use of specially planted instructions at intermediate levels in order to generate test results.

In practice, a compromise is often an effective way forward, with top-down testing using stubs being the predominant method employed, but with critical routines written and tested in parallel through the use of test drivers. Naturally, this mixed approach should not simply happen; the existence of special cases should have been identified at detailed design, and the strategy for their testing outlined in the test plan. This approach will regularly be employed where only part of an existing software system is being replaced: that is, the system is undergoing 'maintenance'. This stage of the development life cycle is considered more fully in Chapter 9.

Black-box or white-box testing

Top-down/bottom-up testing approaches are concerned with a definition of a section, or sections, of code' to be tested. At a rather deeper level, decisions also have to be made about the nature of the test itself: is it to be concerned with *what* that code section does, or *how* it does it?

'What' testing is known as black-box testing. The section under test will be known to perform certain functions in response to certain inputs. It will also be known to produce certain outputs, and to affect known global data items. A black-box test, therefore, will concentrate on the interface between the code section and its surroundings.

'How' testing is known as white-box testing. Given a knowledge of the code section's internal workings – data structures used, code paths and loops employed so as to achieve the functional performance – a white-box test uses this knowledge to exercise code specifics in an attempt to uncover flaws in the program logic.

As the methods are complementary, a code section should be tested by means of both black-box and white-box techniques.

Design of test cases

A test case is a design for a particular test. It will stipulate criteria for the generation of test data, the criteria being tailored according to whether a black-box or a white-box test is being conducted. We consider briefly three of the most common approaches to test case design.

Path (or logic) testing

This is a white-box technique. Its objective is to cause the traversal of a number of different paths through the code under test. Naturally the degree to which this is possible will depend on the complexity of the coding, but general objectives might be execution of every statement at least once, and taking every decision path for true and false conditions. The difficulty of path testing is obviously exacerbated the more complex the code under test is. It may be necessary in practice for the strategy to identify a representative sample of paths if the number of possible combinations is unrealistically high. Path testing is equally applicable to module and integration tests: in the latter case the paths are the links between modules.

Note that, of itself, path testing does not prove that a program will produce the right results. If a path is missing it cannot be traversed by the test, although its absence will cause incorrect results at some time. Path testing should be combined with meaningful data wherever possible.

Boundary and stress testing
This technique tests software at its operational extremes. It is based on the principle that many errors occur at the upper and lower points of a range, and thus aims to test data structures, control flows, and data values just below, at, and just above their supposed maxima and minima. Boundary testing can be used in a variety of situations:

Black-box testing:

- creating empty and full file structures
- input of out-of-range data values, including null input
- attempting invalid operations, e.g. edit non-existent file

White-box testing:

- array handling with subscripts outside declared range
- loops which are executed zero, maximum times
- values for variables with defined limits

In a similar fashion, boundary testing can be used to obtain a measure of performance capability. A real-time system, for instance, would be tested with maxima, e.g. for data transfer rates, as stated in the requirements specification and the system performance measured.

Stress testing, as its name suggests, is performance boundary testing carried to the point at which the software 'gives way'. Using the example of data transfer rates again, a stress test might systematically increase data arrival rates until the system failed through a buffer overflowing or data values being lost. The information gleaned from such a test would be the 'critical value' (in data arrival rate) at which failures begin to occur.

Equivalence (input data) partitioning
This is a black-box technique: its objective is to uncover classes of errors, as opposed to individual errors.

A primary target for this sort of test is the data structure and the coding which manipulates it. By selection of a combination of invalid and valid data sets for input to the routine under test it is argued that a good chance exists for a small group of repeatedly applied test sequences to uncover a number of errors.

Regression testing:
Although not strictly a technique in itself, regression testing does exercise the mind during the testing phases of the software life cycle. As stated at the start of this chapter, a successful test will uncover errors. Once these

errors have been corrected, tests involving regression – 'going back' – must then be carried out on the modified software.

The question to be answered is: how far back do the tests have to go? At the extreme, every test ever conducted on the item of software in question would be repeated; in practice it is usually possible to justify with some confidence a regression test which is a subset of those carried out before. Given that the software is well structured it should really only be necessary to retest the amended module and its interfaces anyway. Once again, the test plan should provide guidelines for regression testing related to the software design.

8.3 Testing techniques and tools

In very broad terms, testing of a program can be conducted in one of two ways: statically – by examination of the program code, or dynamically – through the controlled execution of that code. Both approaches have their place in the scheme of things and, in fact, should be regarded as complementary. Static analysis encourages a critical viewing of what has been produced, thereby discouraging an *ad hoc* 'run it and see how it goes' attitude; dynamic analysis enables code to be examined under conditions which have been specially designed to maximise the possibility of error detection.

Static analysis

Structured walkthroughs
A structured walkthrough involves a checking of program code by a number of experienced people. As a purely manual technique it is often criticised as being time-consuming. Like most things, the time question is relative. A successful walkthrough can often reveal more errors than an automated system. Moreover, no special test software has to be produced and this in itself saves time.

A structured walkthrough (or code inspection) shares much in common with a review meeting, in that it it should be well organised with a chairperson, a secretary and a clearly defined agenda. There are differences however, the major of which are:

- the object to be 'walked through' is an item of some detail – an aspect of design or, more usually, a piece of program coding
- the group will comprise peer group staff for the person whose work is being scrutinised: at this level, programmers and analysts. Since the objective of the walkthrough is to reveal errors it is seen to be

psychologically important that these people are non-threatening; in other words, non-management

- in this respect the members of the group will be expected to take on different roles (such as user, program maintainer, quality assurance representative) for the purposes of the meeting

As with a design review, a structured walkthrough will begin with a presentation of the work by the program author. During this explanation the other members of the group will intervene as necessary to ask for further clarification, or to make constructive criticisms. The walkthrough seeks to identify errors, but not to correct them: that is the programmer's job. It also looks at areas which, although not erroneous in themselves, either contravene sound programming practices or presage future trouble – aspects difficult to automate.

The following is a typical checklist of points to be considered during a structured walkthrough:

- does the coded unit implement all the functions of the detailed design specification? This exercise can also highlight deficiencies in the structuring of the program if it is found that individual functions cannot be clearly traced
- is it easy to cross-refer to the detailed design specification? Somebody else may have to do this one day; examination helps to ease the problems of future maintenance
- are there any logical coding errors? These will often be discovered by the programmer, simply through the process of explaining how the program works. In this respect a major benefit of the walkthrough is that many errors may be uncovered in a single session, rather than through test runs taking place over a relatively long period of time
- is the programming 'defensive', and has this been tested for? Has the programmer included checks for errors which may occur during the execution of the program? These include error conditions specified in the requirements, together with 'internal' checks for particular occurrences as discussed in Chapter 7
- is the program commented adequately? Questioning on this aspect can extend to a walkthrough of any associated documentation if this is appropriate
- have any obscure methods or code been used? Unnecessarily complex or 'trick' programming is to be deplored since it inevitably exacerbates difficulties in future maintenance. This is another aspect of static analysis which is almost impossible to automate
- has the programmer justified the use of any low-level code inserts? As we have seen in Chapter 7, machine-language or assembly-

language coding is a form of obscure programming that will sometimes have to be employed – but only for good reason

Automated static analysis

A static analysis tool will operate by conducting one or more passes of all,
or part, of a program's source code structure. Its objectives will be twofold:
to highlight errors and to produce statistical information for the programmer to use.

The compiler, for instance, in performing a translation of source code to
object code, necessarily conducts a certain amount of static analysis.
Statements which do not conform to the syntax rules of the source language are flagged, and error messages produced. This is the most common
form of static analysis operation performed on the source code; unfortunately it tends too often to be the only one, out of the many possibilities
that exist.

Static analysis tools provide the wherewithal for a number of helpful
operations to be carried out on the source code. Referring to the trivial
Pascal program of Figure 8.3, such operations might cover the following
areas:

Analysis of control flow

Through a representation of the code in the form of a directed graph or
similar structure, the various possible execution paths are presented. (In
Figure 8.3 the single entry into line 12 would diverge into three successive
dual paths reflecting the three conditional statements at lines 13, 15 and
17.) In this way potential trouble areas such as unreachable code sections
or procedures with multiple entry/exit points as well as poorly structured
code in general can be identified.

Analysis of data flow

This is rather more than a listing of data declarations and appearances of
data references within the source code. Data flow analysis involves
examining these items within the overall context of the program, so as to
identify such things as the use of uninitialised variables (e.g. the reference
to C2 in line 14 of Figure 8.3 were line 8 to be omitted), mixing of
real/integer data items in expressions and as far as flagging potential errors
or inconsistencies such as successive assignments to a variable without its
being used in between.

Analysis of information flow

An extension of data flow analysis, information flow analysis aims to link
together all program inputs with program outputs so as to show how the
latter are derived from the former (e.g. the reference to C5 in line 22 would

```
LINE STMT

1                    PROGRAM TRIVIA(INPUT, OUTPUT);
2
3                    VAR
4                    C2, C3, C5: INTEGER;
5                    I: INTEGER;
6
7      1             BEGIN
8      2                 C2 := 0;
9      3                 C3 := 0;
10     4                 C5 := 0;
11     5                 FOR I := 1 TO 1000 DO
12                           BEGIN
13     6                         IF I MOD 2 = 0 THEN
14     7                             C2 := C2 + 1;
15     8                         IF I MOD 3 = 0 THEN
16     9                             C3 := C3 ; C2;
17     10                        IF I MOD 5 = 0 THEN
18     11                            C5 := C5 + C2
19                           END;
20     12                WRITELN(C2);
21     13                WRITELN(C3);
22     14                WRITELN(C5);
23                    END.
```

Figure 8.3. Pascal program

be linked to its dependence on both itself (lines 10,18) and C2 (line 18)). Not only does this make apparent erroneous steps in such activities as formula evaluation but, through the construction of a dependency matrix, it gives clear assistance towards those variables that need to be the focus of attention in the definition of test cases.

Semantic analysis
Semantic analysis tools aim to identify the various paths through the program code (e.g. passing from line 13 to line 19 in Figure 8.3 involves eight possible paths). This information, of course, is just what is needed in designing white-box tests for the code in question.

Symbolic execution
Taken a stage further, information flow analysis and semantic analyis result in symbolic execution: the traversal of identified paths so as to build up a

picture of which variables have their values affected by what execution path (e.g. the path 13,14,15,17,19 and its affect on variables I and C2). This type of analysis furnishes more information for future testing – in this case a clear indication of what results might be expected for a particular test case.

Program documentation

Each of the static analyses mentioned produces output – in the form of procedure summaries, cross-reference listing, path traces, etc. – which augment the documentary information associated with the software under development. This sort of information is invaluable, both during the development stages and, much later, when software maintenance needs to be carried out from it. The fact that it is virtually impossible to produce by hand, at least in any volume, and so easy to produce by computer in itself is an argument for static analysis tools.

There is still considerable potential for development in this area. Given the IPSE ethos outlined in Chapter 7, it is desirable that such progress be made. Thorne (1987a, b) lists some of the possibilities:

- upward links to formal specification techniques so that assertions may be generated at the lower module levels
- automatic generation of test data sets
- direct links to test environments (e.g. dynamic analysers – see below)
- automation of refinement loops
- compact graphical presentation of analysis data
- semi-automated help facilities

Automatic dynamic analysis

Dynamic analysis involves the production of information during, and after, the execution of the program under test. Three separate activities need to take place.

First, the program must be instrumented – that is, augmented in some way with statements which will cause information about the program and its data to be produced whilst execution is taking place. The simplest, and least convenient, way of doing this is for the programmer to carry out this task by means of a liberal scattering of output statements into key areas. Much preferred, however, is for this instrumentation process itself to be automated. This can be achieved by extended forms of the static analysis tools just discussed through, for instance, the path analysis function being extended to selectively instrument some of the code paths which it identifies. This, of course, requires the instrumentation code to be compiled along with the source program. A translation system which can handle optional compilation of instrumentation statements is invaluable, since it allows dynamic analysis to be turned on or off easily without the need to edit those statements out of the program's source code.

Second, the program is executed with chosen test cases and dynamic analysis data produced. A variety of methods are needed. Interactive mode operation, of course, but also an option of batch operation – where a soak test is concerned, for instance, or a simulation. Options should also be available with regard to printing of results collected from a test run and also its storage in disc files.

The third aspect of the process is the analysis itself. For interactive operation, much of the analysis will be done during execution. Wherever possible, however, output should also be generated which can be examined at length. If this is printed material then it should be in terms that the programmer can assimilate quickly, not in the form of a hexadecimal memory dump. This still requires that analysis be conducted by a programmer, however. Sending the data to a file (quite often in addition to printing) means that, with suitably designed tools, a certain amount of the analysis itself can be automated.

Broadly speaking, dynamic analysis generates information classified in one of two ways: trace information, or execution summary information.

Trace information is generated as the program is executed; it provides historic details. A good dynamic analysis tool will offer a variety of trace options:

- variable tracing: output of data values associated with nominated identifiers and/or data structures whenever those values change
- flow tracing: identification of statements or statement groups (such as procedures) as they are executed
- selective tracing: automatic inhibition of trace output whenever a selected code area is entered (detailed tracing would not be needed when executing a trusted library routine, for instance)
- information tracing: parameter value information on entry to/exit from nominated statement groups, such as procedures and library routines
- assertion tracing: evaluation of certain algebraic conditions at key points in the program so as to verify certain logical assumptions about a program's general well-being, e.g. that, at a certain point in a program, a particular boolean flag is set correctly

Execution summary information, as its name suggests, collects together information which has been gathered during execution and presents it in summary form. Thus, each of the trace information categories above could have a summary generated for it: a usage summary of entries to/exits from a particular procedure, for instance.

As a simple example, Figure 8.4 shows a summarised path analysis for the core of the Pascal program of Figure 8.3, with the values in the left-hand column being the number of times that the statement on that line was executed.

```
COUNT  LINE STMT
             :
             :
    1     7    1        BEGIN
    1     8    2          C2 := 0;
    1     9    3          C3 := 0;
    1    10    4          C5 := 0;
    1    11    5          FOR I := 1 TO 1000 DO
         12               BEGIN
 1000    13    6          IF I MOD 2 = 0 THEN
  500    14    7            C2 := C2 + 1;
 1000    15    8          IF I MOD 3 = 0 THEN
  333    16    9            C3 := C3 ; C2;
 1000    17   10          IF I MOD 5 = 0 THEN
  200    18   11            C5 := C5 + C2
             :
             :
```

Figure 8.4. Path analysis

By reference to such a summary it is possible to see immediately if, for instance, some statements are not being executed at all – indicating either a poor test case, or perhaps a logical error which is preventing such statements being executed. Another use would be in boundary testing for performance. If the program needs to be speeded up, a knowledge of which statement groups are called most frequently enables recoding for maximising efficiency to be accurately focused.

As with static analysis tools, there is still considerable potential for development in this area. Thorne (1987a, b) suggests:

- integration, or combination, of dynamic assertion techniques with the proof of correctness employed in static analysis
- auto-generation of dynamic assertion statements
- auto-adaption, or generation, of test cases
- application of dynamic analysis techniques to memory critical embedded software
- application of dynamic analysis techniques to discontinuous code (e.g. interrupt-driven systems)
- program timing analysis

Once again, progress with IPSE design is seen as the ideal medium through which to implement such developments. Static and dynamic analysis tools overlap in so many ways that to combine them within a common environment will provide the most natural way of conducting all aspects of software testing.

9 Acceptance and Maintenance

9.1 Acceptance

The point at which the quality of a software product receives approval is that of acceptance: after all, who – knowingly, at least – would take delivery of a product that is of inferior quality? Acceptance testing is therefore a key stage in the software development life cycle. Once passed and put into active service, the said software will not only cause embarrassment and inconvenience should it need to be put right, it may also cost a customer much in financial terms.

An element of testing is inevitable, therefore. But testing which is, in one important respect, different to that which has gone before. Until this stage – as Sommerville (1985) points out – all testing is carried out by the organisation resonsible for constructing the system. Acceptance testing is the process of testing the system with real data, the information which the system is intended to manipulate. The process of acceptance testing often demonstrates errors in the system requirements definition. The requirements may not reflect the actual facilities and performance required by the user, and acceptance testing may demonstrate that the system does not exhibit the intended performance and functionality.

Thus, acceptance testing is the responsibility of the customer. It can range from nothing – reflecting complete, but possibly misplaced, trust in the contractor – to exhaustive testing. Effort expended in this area is not cheap and the temptation not to spend yet more money on what may well have been an already very expensive exercise is quite overwhelming. Such inaction will invariably prove to be a false economy; investments of time and money in acceptance testing will pay for themselves in ensuring a trouble-free life when the system goes into operation.

Traditionally an acceptance test focuses on the capabilities of the software product, covering two aspects:

- functionality: does the system do what is required?
- performance: does it carry out those functions, e.g. within any time constraints?

These aspects are covered in more detail below. However it would seem essential, given all that has been said so far concerning quality assurance and control, that acceptance procedures should extend beyond the software to encompass the documentation associated with that software.

It should be unnecessary to go through the vast numbers of documents involved in a major development. Suffice it to say that if the design, code and test documentation, along with more obvious literature such as user manuals and operations manuals, is of inadequate quality, then operation of the system and/or its maintenance will inevitably pose problems in the future. Acceptance of documentation is an important activity and should be accorded the time and effort it deserves (and which good documentation will save).

Acceptance of functionality

The fact that the term 'demonstration test' is often used instead of the term 'acceptance test' is an indication that functionality is the primary, and sometimes only, concern.

Shooman (1983) gives details of a typical, three-stage, acceptance test sequence:

Stage 1: Feature check
The contractor is required to demonstrate that each of the features of the system works properly by running one test case for each feature. These test cases will have been defined in either the original contract or in subsequent documents available to both contractor and customer.

Stage 2: Comprehensive check
The customer supplies a set of test cases which are unknown to the contractor. This set will usually include the boundaries of each feature and any known stressful points, as well as a distribution of values over the range of inputs.

Stage 3: Extraordinary-input check
The customer supplies a set of test cases which probe to see how the system responds to input values outside the normal range, to garbage input, to input data in the wrong form or sequence, etc. Any anomalous behaviour from that specified in the contract is deemed a failure.

In this way confidence is achieved that the system behaves in conformance with its requirements specification. Note that there are two implications of failure at this level, depending on the cause of failure:

- Failures due to non-conformance with the requirements specification are the responsibility of the contractor; the customer (hopefully at the contractual stage) will have specified what the consequences of failing any stage of the acceptance tests are, and the contractor is bound to solving the problems so identified.

- Failures due to inadequate requirements specification are laid at the customer's door (hence the importance of quality requirements) and separate negotiation will need to take place regarding what is to be done about them. The choice for the customer is stark: either pay the contractor more money to solve the problem, or leave the fault in place and live with it.

Note that the testing approaches outlined in Chapter 8 apply equally well to the derivation of acceptance test cases. From this it will be seen that acceptance test design takes effort. The customer must decide on the level of investment in this respect, bearing in mind that inadequate acceptance testing may well let a contractor off a very big hook.

Acceptance of performance

Performance measurement criteria
Every system will, to a greater or lesser extent, need to undergo acceptance testing for performance as well as functionality. Criteria for system performance requirements will have been specified; the problem now is in assessing the performance level of the finished product to determine its level of conformity with this aspect of the initial requirements. The aim, as with functional acceptance, will be either to accept or to reject: acceptance through satisfactory performance (where 'satisfactory' may, of course, be less than the original requirement), or rejection because of an unsatisfactory performance – in which case the contractor will be heading back to the drawing board to try to remedy the situation.

Performance testing will necessarily be influenced by which definition of 'performance' is being employed. As a basis for discussion, we use the following general definition:

'performance is defined as the probability of a computer system completing a given throughput of work in a given period of time'.

Such a definition, which applies equally well to both real-time and batch systems, suggests that performance is influenced by four major factors:

- the system's intrinsic hardware/software capabilities
- the workload applied to the system
- the planning, scheduling and loading of work on the system
- the efficiency of the system operations staff

No contractor would agree to be assessed by a mechanism which incorporated the last two points since these are beyond his control. Their influence on system performance in practice should not be underestimated, however.

It is in consideration of intrinsic capabilites and workload that performance acceptance tests are concentrated. Two broad units of measure are employed: throughput and delay. Throughput is a measure of the rate at which a defined unit of work can be performed (what constitutes a unit of work is, of course, peculiar to the application area; a complex system handling different types of work may require a number of different measures). It might be thought that this one measure would be sufficient. This is not the case. Most systems will be subjected to varying loads – from nil to overload – and a consideration of throughput alone will not tell the customer how the system responds at extremes of loading. Thus, figures for throughput are simultaneously linked to measurements for delay; in other words, acceptance is generally tied to a requirement for a particular throughput at a particular level of delay, with average and maximum figures usually being quoted.

Within an ideal computer system a balance is achieved between demands of the workload on one hand and the system's resources on the other, with fluctuations in activity being smoothed by optimal scheduling on the part of the system software. This ideal may not be achieved, however, for many reasons: the workload may vary too widely, scheduling may not be optimal, systems resources may be inappropriately configured, and so on. For this reason performance measurements must be taken through test runs conducted with the system running in a manner which mirrors as closely as possible the mode in which the system will be working when in full operation.

Performance testing should focus on those areas which invariably exert most influence on system performance. There are three, each a combination of hardware/software risk:

Processing capacity. This is determined by the actual hardware processing speed coupled with the software processing that needs to be carried out. Delay time will naturally increase as the processing load increases. A cpu-bound system – that is, one within which delay times are primarily a function of the processor's speed – is less susceptible to the improving of its performance through purely software-based methods. Often the addition of another processor (assuming that this is technically possible) is the only solution. It is crucial to determine, however, that the load being imposed on the processor is user-generated. It is not unknown for computer processors to spend more time executing their own operating system software than doing real work. Where this is found to be the case, perhaps through poor scheduling or store management algorithms, then some system 'tuning' should be possible to improve matters.

Memory capacity. It is a constant surprise to some people that memory allocation can so influence performance as to bring a system virtually to its knees. The problem area is that of 'swapping' – the transfer of memory areas to and from backing store so as to provide the capability of executing a program (or, more accurately, a number of programs) with a total memory requirement in excess of that physically available. Inadequate methods and algorithms either for allocation, or determining which areas should be swapped out at any moment, can lead to quite horrendous levels of 'thrashing', in which a system spends more of its time swapping than in executing programs. Again, this situation, most often caused by a set of circumstances in which a system unwisely takes on more user demand than it can handle, should be detected by good acceptance testing and 'tuning' carried out as a consequence.

Input/output capacity. Peripheral-bound systems have their delay time unduly influenced by the speed at which peripheral devices are able to work. This is invariably the case with commercial data processing systems, for instance, but not necessarily in a way that presents problems; the acceptable delay time for executing a payroll program may well be measured in hours. Where problems may occur is in the unbalanced use of equipment – such as the allocation of too many disc drives to a single controller, for instance – or in cases where inadequate communications speeds coupled with slow-running software and/or too-small memory buffers causes loss of data. Acceptance testing at peak, as well as average, data transfer rates will highlight any problems in this area.

The assumption in each of the above cases is, of course, that performance is actually measurable.

Performance measurement techniques
Extracting performance information from a system can be done in a variety of ways, either singly or in combination. The four approaches below are representative.

Benchmarking. A benchmark 'program' is a fixed and well-defined amount of work capable of being run on the system under test. As the results obtained should reflect the way in which the system actually processes the work, it is self-evident that the benchmark should be representative of the projected workload. This implies that time must be spent in conducting an analysis of an existing workload.

The time taken in constructing a benchmark is a major factor in its design. Various options are open to reduce a very lengthy process to one which is merely lengthy. For example, one can construct a 'representative' benchmark by taking a set of programs from an existing workload and converting them as necessary. Clearly this is not an available option for a new system. Alternatively, one might construct a 'synthetic' benchmark: that is, develop a program which is able to display 'representative behaviour' – in terms of processing and input/output levels, for instance – not through meaningful instruction sequences but through parameterised loops of sets of instruction types. Although it sounds attractive, this approach inevitably gives rise to doubts about whether or not the synthetic workload really does provide an accurate representation of the actual workload.

More simply, one can use a 'standard' benchmark. Lots exist, such as:

- Whetstone: a mid-1970s derived benchmark based on a floating-point instruction mix
- Dhrystone: integer-based equivalent to Whetstone, although not as widely accepted
- TP 1 and ET 1: two comparable methods for measuring the transaction processing speeds of on-line transaction processing systems
- Livermore loops: a set of test programs for measuring the speed and efficiency of vector processors
- Gabriel triangle: a test for use with parallel architectures

Software monitoring. The system is inspected on a regular basis by 'sampler' program which uses minimal resources. On each activation it reads values from 'system meters' – counters maintained by the operating system – from which it can calculate and output absolute or average utilisations of machine resources such as cpu loading, store occupancy, disc accesses, etc. in the time interval since its last activation. This process, essentially a holistic performance measure, can be refined to provide measures for the execution of a particular job or sub-system.

Software monitoring is relatively cheap to implement and run, and will provide a wealth of information for analysis. Its major disadvantage is that it is sometimes impractical to use in the measurement of time-critical systems (such as embedded control systems) in which the cpu loading imposed by the monitor itself becomes significant enough to invalidate the measurements.

Hardware monitoring. Hardware monitoring is used to discover the performance characteristics of a system when it is not feasible to use a software monitor. Usually taking the form of a micro/minicomputer with an associated tape or disc drive, the monitor collects performance data in bit form. The target computer is attached to the monitor by a number of high-impedance probes inserted at points where cpu, channel and peripheral activity may be sampled. The data so obtained is analysed after a monitoring session by a suitable program which converts the results to graphical form.

The advantage of hardware monitoring is that the results it produces are very accurate, since the monitor does not influence in any way the operation of the target system. Its disadvantages are cost, and the requirement for specialist staff to interpret the measurement data.

Emulation. Emulation provides for the replacement of a working system component by a monitoring system which exhibits the same external characteristics as the component it replaces. Two examples will illustrate the approach.

Testing the performance of a multi-terminal computer system could be carried out by using a terminal emulator: a system which runs on a separate computer with its own disc store and which, in operation, acts exactly as would a collection of terminals. The disc would hold 'scripts' of transactions looking, as far as the host system is concerned, exactly like the real thing. Outputs from the host would be taken by the emulator and recorded on disc. In addition, measurement information – transaction start and finish time, active terminals, etc. – would be recorded. A major advantage in this case would be that something like varying the number of on-line terminals could be achieved through changing a single parameter. No real operators would ever need to be recruited.

A terminal emulator such as that described automates something that could be achieved manually, albeit in a highly time-consuming manner. Emulation of the environment surrounding an embedded system (that is, a system not having direct operator input/output), on the other hand, makes possible something which could not easily be done in any other way. The task of proving that a nuclear power station process control system will perform its time-critical functions would be virtually impossible without some form of emulator.

Resource utilisation. Much of what has been said above has a direct bearing on the topic of resource utilisation. The requirements specification for many software systems will decree, typically, that the final product should have 50% spare capacity in processor, memory and input/output. That is, that the software should be able to 'grow' to require half again as much resource as in the delivered system, without exceeding the capacity of the hardware. (Although, as Evans and Marciniak (1987) point out, confusion exists surrounding the interpretation of this requirement. Contractors often argue that it means they must preserve capacity for 50% growth – that is, they can utilise 66% of the resource leaving 33% (50% of 66%) spare. This ambiguity can be resolved by quoting 100% spare if the requirement is that only half of the available resource is to be used by the contractor.)

Most software systems 'expand' over a period of time. The performance monitoring and measuring techniques described above should therefore not only be employed as part of the acceptance procedure but also throughout the lifetime of the software product. In this way it will be possible to prevent a gradual deterioration of performance and provide statistical evidence to support, for example, expansion of the hardware.

9.2 Metrics

Carefully designed and conducted, the acceptance test should ensure that the final product conforms to its specification in both functionality and performance. But how about quality?

The acceptance of the finished article implies acceptance on the part of the customer that it is of a satisfactory quality. If quality control and assurance methods have been rigorously applied throughout the system life cycle, of course, then the quality aspect should be beyond doubt. In accepting functionality and performance, however, the customer usually has evidence to point to in the form of figures and results – sometimes more than he would wish. Software metrics seek to provide quantitative data, throughout the development life cycle, upon which the customer can base acceptance of quality.

Software metrics is a study of numerical measures which can be applied to the products and processes of software development. In quality terms, metrics fall into two broad categories: those that aim to predict software quality, and those that test software quality. Within these categories exist a bewildering variety of methods – none of which, it must be said, has been welcomed by the software community as being an infallible guide to quality.

Predictive metrics, as their name suggests, are employed during the early stages of the development cycle so as to give an indication of how well the final product will exhibit quality characteristics. Thus a high value for a metric such as 'structuredness' would be taken as a strong predictor that the eventual program code will exhibit a correspondingly high degree of maintainability.

Test metrics, on the other hand, are employed 'after the event' – at the implementation (or, more commonly, the post-implementation) stage. Counting decision statements in the final program code, for instance, is one way of assessing complexity – another factor in the question of how maintainable a piece of software will prove to be.

The fundamental questions, whichever category is being considered, are what to measure, and how? In a book of this size it is impossible to deal with these questions in any depth. Not only are the numbers of candidate metrics enormous, but most have strong relationships with other metrics and are capable of varying interpretation. We therefore attempt nothing more ambitious than to give the flavour of metrication through reference to the seminal works of Boehm (1980) and McCall (1977).

Boehm's approach is based on the use of what might be termed yes/no metrics. Metrics for structuredness, for instance:

- have the rules for transfer of control between modules been followed?
- are the modules limited in size?
- do all the subprograms contain at most one point of exit?
- do all subprograms and functions have only one entry point?
- is the program written in a standard set of constructs?

An empirical cost–benefit study was used to evaluate the usefulness of these metrics. This was based on a process of investigating error types, the development stage at which the error originated, and at which stage and by application of which metric that error might have been detected. In this highly subjective manner, and through an approach concentrated heavily on one aspect (error occurrence), a metric set was defined. As a result, the use of Boehm's work suggests that checklists and standards-type metrics allow inferences to be drawn which vary from a 'warm feeling' that good practices of software production have been employed through to a good level of confidence that certain classes of error do not exist in the final software product.

McCall's approach aimed at providing measurements rather than check-lists. Thus, whereas Boehm asks 'do all subprograms contain at most one point of exit?'. McCall would evaluate:

$$\text{Metric} = \frac{\text{no. of subprograms containing at most one point of exit}}{\text{total no. of subprograms}}$$

Adjustment was conducted, as appropriate, so that values close to 1 were indicative of high quality, those close to 0 low quality. McCall's method also derived operational 'ratings' which aimed to facilitate a judgement over the final quality of the product, e.g.

$$\text{Rating} = 1 - \frac{\text{no. of lines in error after start of formal testing}}{\text{no. of source code lines, less comments}}$$

The empirical evaluation method employed sought to establish a quality rating factor at both system and module levels through examining systems for which data was available on both development and operational use, using regression techniques to establish the relationship between metrics and quality factor ratings.

Code metrics are typical of such measures since it is clearly possible to extract 'feature' counts from an examination of a program's code. For instance, McCall-like metrics could be based on:

- executable lines of code (where 'line' is variously interpreted as ranging from something like a Pascal statement to a COBOL verb). Used to assess a program's size, form ratios of subprogram lengths, error lines with non-error lines, etc.
- decision density: a count of decision statements per n lines of code, giving an indication of a program's complexity (more decisions imply greater complexity) and, thereby, its understandability
- function density: a count of subprogram/function calls per n lines of code, giving a measure of the modularity (or structuredness)
- transformation counts: the number of statements which change the value of one or more data items. Used to generate a ratio of transformations per n lines of code and, thereby, a feel (where too many transformation statements exist) for an inadequate use of subprograms
- input/output counts: again as a ratio with n lines of code to show how well machine-dependent aspects have been isolated (thus, a measure of portability)
- comment counts: against total lines of code to provide a measure of a program's self-documentedness

This approach, and those which have followed its principles, provide an objective technique for evaluating metrics. They do, however, depend on being able to identify ratings for quality factors and on the assumption, possibly misplaced, that the underlying data is suited to statistical analysis. A value in the range 0 to 1 does not guarantee accuracy regarding quality.

For instance, by examining a number of completed projects it is clearly possible to establish a baseline figure for, say, the number of code lines expected to be generated in providing a menu facility. Less-than-baseline values derived from assessing a current project might mean:

- poor coding: a low number of lines caused through errors of omission
- good coding: a low number of lines because of efficient programming
- average coding: because the menu facility provides fewer functions than those from which the baseline was derived

And these without considering the different programming abilities of the staff working on the projects! Interpretation, then, is all-important. In fact it is difficult to foresee a situation in which this will not be the case. No two software systems are the same, almost by definition, and thus measures which attempt to equate the two will inevitably require some form of judgement by a referee.

Clearly, this problem is exacerbated where very few other systems exist for comparative purposes. In fact a major difficulty in this area has not been in deciding what data to collect, but in overcoming the practical difficulties of actually collecting such data. The concept of an IPSE, as described in Chapters 6 and 7, should change this situation. Given that the IPSE, by definition, has access to all elements of a software product, from initial design through to final code, incorporation of software metrics into IPSEs is an obvious step.

For instance, Kitchenham and McDermid (1986) suggest that IPSEs may automatically be be able to extract a number of design metrics such as fan-in, fan-out and interconnectivity measures from the product representation. During the later stages of development, additional measures of the testing activity, such as test metrics, and information about code execution behaviour, such as time between failures, may be available.

IPSEs should also provide some basic facilities – simple tabular or graphical – for analysing the collected data. Given the concepts of PCTE for common interfaces between an IPSE and other tools this data should also be accessible from other commercial packages (such as cost models) and user-written analysis tools. It could well be that IPSE developments will mean that the time for software metrics has finally come.

9.3 Maintenance

Figures abound to show that software maintenance is an horrendous task. Speaking at the inaugural meeting of the Centre for Software Maintenance at Durham University, US expert Kent Peterson said that in the 1960s the effort of maintaining software represented 30% of the programming task; in 1985 it amounted to 85% of the task.

Other speakers suggested that total US spending on maintenance of software amounted to about 2% of the country's gross national product; and that the US federal government, owners of 25 billion lines of code, spends 23% of its total information technology budget on the maintenance of that code.

Before looking at why this, the final stage of the software development cycle, assumes such massive proportions it is necessary to define what is meant by the term 'software maintenance'.

The four classes of maintenance

This is an illuminating exercise in itself, for we see that 'maintenance' in this context is a gross abuse of the meaning of that word. It does not simply mean the replacement of a defective part by a 'new' one – the accepted meaning of the word when applied to, say, the maintenance of a motor vehicle. Rather, as Pressman (1982) points out, it is used as an umbrella term to cover four different levels of activity:

Correction

Equivalent to the replacing of defective parts, corrective maintenance involves the diagnosis and correction of latent errors in the software system.

Adaption

Involves the changing of the software system to 'keep pace' with changes in its operating environment. New peripheral devices, for instance, with different input/output interfaces will require software changes even though the old software was working perfectly. Similarly, new versions of an underlying operating system might require adaptive maintenance to be carried out.

Perfection

The price of success. Software which is well received and widely used will inevitably promote demands that it be 'improved' by the addition of further facilities. Perfective maintenance is concerned with satisfying those demands: with extending, again, a program that is by definition working very well!

Prevention

An activity which replaces a working program by another which appears to work in exactly the same way! Strange as it may seem, this is an activity that is likely to increase, since it involves the changing of software for the purposes of producing a version which can more easily be subjected to adaptive or perfective maintenance in the future. An obvious example is the rewriting of a badly unstructured program so that it becomes structured. As IPSEs become widely accepted more preventive maintenance will be conducted as packages are changed in order to be capable of running within such an environment.

The observer might suggest that the reason software maintenance consumes such a high proportion of resources is simply because the four distinct activities of correction, adaption, perfection and prevention are lumped together under the one term 'maintenance'. Certainly this forms part of the reason; but only part. The fact remains that it is in the maintenance arena that many problems occur, whichever of the four categories of work is in progress, and it is in the resolution of these problems that the bulk of the total cost is incurred.

The problems with maintenance

Lientz *et al.* (1976) conducted a major survey and reported on 24 problem areas for software maintenance activities. This list is reproduced below; it is in descending order of trouble, the problems at the top occurring more frequently than those lower down. Although compiled over ten years ago, the survey is, unfortunately, still relevant today. For this reason each entry is annotated as a convenient way of pointing out the potential sources of maintenance problems. Many, as will be seen, arise directly from a lack of quality in the software product – in other words, they are avoidable.

(a) User demands for enhancements, extensions: perfective maintenance, that is. Caused by popularity, as was pointed out above, but very often through inadequate requirements specification. The use of such techniques as prototyping and 4GLs aims to keep this problem down to a minimum.

(b) Quality of system documentation: no change can be made to a piece of software until the 'maintainer' has discovered what that software is supposed to do. The longer this takes the higher the maintenance cost becomes. Poor-quality documentation inevitably extends discovery time.

(c) Competing demands on maintenance personnel time: organisations which fail to recognise software maintenance as an activity in its own right do not employ specialised maintenance staff. Consequently, development staff, having moved on to other work, then have to be switched back to maintenance tasks with a consequent loss of productivity.

(d) Quality of original programs: unstructured code, 'trick' programming, programs out of step with their associated documentation. They cause a maintenance programmer to spend longer than necessary climbing the learning curve.

(e) Meeting scheduled commitments: similar to (c) in many ways. Errors do not manifest themselves at convenient times, and their removal cannot wait. Staff are, thereby, moved into corrective maintenance with a consequent affect on their scheduled commitments.

(f) Lack of user understanding of system: 'red herrings'. A percentage of reported errors will not be errors at all, but result from the fact that the software is being used incorrectly. Maintenance costs are still incurred, of course, since the report has to be investigated – though item (b), poor documentation, may mean that the developer is really to blame anyway.

(g) Availability of maintenance program personnel: maintenance is, by definition, an 'after-the-event' activity. If a problem arises some years after the software was written the originator may no longer be available. Other staff will take longer to find out how the software works.

(h) Adequacy of system design specifications: quality controls at the design level seek to ensure that the design is well structured, with interfaces clearly defined. Adaptive maintenance, for instance, is made much more difficult if this is not the case.

(i) Turnover of maintenance personnel: maintenance programming has a 'Cinderella' image, with staff involved often feeling that their role is inferior to that of development staff, who are working on new and exciting projects. Staff turnover is high, with the result that one program may be successively maintained by many different people.

(j) Unrealistic user expectations: perfective maintenance taken on with little or no regard for the volume of work involved. Often caused through the maintenance role being investigated after, rather than before, the work is taken on.

(k) Processing time of system: as additional functionality is introduced through perfective maintenance, increased demand is placed on system resources. This is often reflected in a performance degradation, with resultant dissatisfaction on the user's part.

(l) Forecasting personnel requirements: a by-product of the difficulty in estimating the magnitude of any maintenance task is that of assessing how many staff are needed to carry out the work.

(m) Skills of maintenance personnel: related to point (i), the poor image of maintenance work regularly leads to its being allocated to trainee members of staff 'to cut their teeth on'. This is counter-productive since delays ensue, further faults creep into the software which has been 'maintained' and, in the worst cases, experienced staff have to be brought in to bail out the project.

(n) Changes to hardware and software: adaptive maintenance. An inevitable activity, given the continuing development of hardware and software. It should therefore be anticipated as an ongoing cost rather than come as a complete surprise.

(o) Budgetary pressures: fixed-price maintenance contracts can cause a severe problem if the magnitude of a task is underestimated. This is more likely to occur, of course, when the original software product lacks quality.

(p) Adherence to programming standards in maintenance: the temptation to cut corners, especially with corrective maintenance, when the pressure is on can mean that the well-developed product gradually disappears under a welter of 'quick fixes'.

(q) Data integrity: or, rather, a lack of it. Badly structured software, in which global variables abound, inevitably results in a change in one area causing something untoward (a 'side-effect' as it is termed) to happen in another.

(r) Motivation of maintenance personnel: excitement for the

programmer is generated by new challenges, not old. Software
maintenance is thus a 'stepping-stone' activity, a necessary period of
boredom between high-octane developments.

(s) Application failures: errors of logic rather than interpretation, in
which, for example, an algorithm has been incorrectly coded.
Ideally, this sort of problem should not occur. That it does is
indicative of inadequate testing or, perhaps, ambiguity in requirements specification.

(t) Maintenance programming productivity: failing to live up to the
level of code generation achieved during the original software
development stages. Not so much a problem, more an unreasonable
expectation. There is an inevitable learning-curve element in any
maintenance task. Until the essential background work has been
completed, code cannot and should not be produced.

(u) Software reliability: clearly a reflection of the number of errors
which remain in the software post-operation. Adequate testing
should keep this number to a minimum. However, software
reliability is also linked to hardware reliability. Requirements for
contingency handling should have been specified and implemented.
If this has not been done then any hardware failure will be reflected
in a corresponding 'crash' in the software.

(v) Storage requirements: as with (k), maintenance activities may cause
additional demands to be made on memory requirements (for extra
code, for instance). This may result in extra work being needed to
'squeeze' the new software system into the old memory space. This
should not prove critical if sensible figures for spare capacity have
been stipulated in the requirements specification.

(w) Management support of system: software maintenance tends to
result not in the production of completely new versions of a complete system, but in parts of the system: 'updates', as they are
known. An updated system is thus generated by incorporating the
new with those old parts which have not been altered in any way.
This is a process fraught with danger – a danger which is greatly
increased if no management support facilities exist. A manual system build can perpetuate an incorrect set of modules through a
number of subsequent versions.

(x) Lack of user interest in system: new software versions are usually
sent to the customer to implement. If the customer is not made
aware that their role has to be carried out accurately and regularly,
then the maintenance can be conducted with all the skill and
reliability in the world and problems will still ensue.

As a study of the above problems reveals, many can be avoided if adequate precautions are taken. The key is in recognising software as a system element that will inevitably undergo change. If this happens then it is much more likely that maintainable software – software possessing the attribute of maintainability – will be produced.

Maintainability

As a final note on this topic it needs to be stressed that maintainability is a multi-dimensional concept, viewed differently by software producers and software users.

Maintainability, as far as a user is concerned, is reflected in the time taken to deal with, for instance, the rectification of any reported error. A well-maintained system will process such reports in the shortest elapsed time. The maintainability metrics of Gilb (1979) indicate those attributes of the maintenance activity which can be quantified so as to provide user's eye figures for the maintainability level of a software system:

- problem recognition time: e.g. verifying the user's claim
- administrative delay time: e.g. filling in the forms
- maintenance tools collection time: e.g. unearthing test harnesses, etc. written for the original project
- problem analysis time: deciding which out of a number of options will best solve the problem
- change specification time: defining the solution, using the standards and procedures previously followed
- active correction time: includes programming, editing, compilation and system building
- local testing time: verifying that the immediate problem has been solved
- global testing time: verifying, probably through regression testing, that no side-effects exist when the new software is merged with the old
- maintenance review time: obtaining authority to issue the new software
- total recovery time: implementation and testing in the field

The software producer, on the other hand, is concerned less with time than with the effort (equivalent to cost) that has to be expended in dealing with an incident report. Maintainability from the producer's perspective is suggested by the environmental factors identified by Kopetz (1979):

- availability of qualified software staff
- understandable system structure
- ease of system handling

- use of standardised programming languages
- use of standardised operating systems
- standardised structure of documentation
- availability of test cases
- built-in debugging facilities
- availability of a proper computer to conduct maintenance

These factors, of course, correlate very well with the maintenance problem areas identified earlier in this chapter. They also, if followed, clearly lead to a reduction in the maintenance-time factors detailed above.

Maintainability is, *par excellence*, a yardstick by which the quality of software can be judged. Paradoxical as it may seem, software that has been developed with a view to being changed is likely to need changing less than any other. It will be quality software.

Bibliography

ANSI/ASQC (1978). A3–1978.

ANSI/IEEE (1983). *IEEE Standard for Software Configuration Management Plans*, ANSI/IEEE Std 828–1983.

ANSI/IEEE (1981). *IEEE Standard for Software Quality Assurance Plans*, ANSI/IEEE Std 730-1981.

Balzer, R. (1985). A 15 year perspective on automatic programming. *IEEE Transactions on Software Engineering*, SE–11, 1254–1268.

Barnes, J.G.P. (1984). *Programming in Ada*. Addison-Wesley.

Beierle, C., Olthoff, W. and Voss, A. (1986). Towards a formalization of the software development process. *Software Engineering 86* (eds D. Barnes and P.J. Brown) Peter Peregrinus, London, pp.130–44.

Bersoff, E. H., Henderson, V. D. and Seigel, S. G. (1980). *Software Configuration Management*. Prentice-Hall, Englewood Cliffs, NJ.

Boehm, B. W., Brown, J. R., Kaspar, H., Lipow, M., Macleod, G. J. and Merrit, M. J. (1980). *Characteristics of Software Quality*. North-Holland, Amsterdam.

Born, G. (1986). Controlling software quality, *Software Engineering* 1, pp.24–28.

Brooks, F.P. Jr. (1986). No silver bullet – essence and accidents of software engineering. *Information Processing '86* (ed. H.-J. Kugler), Elsevier/North-Holland, Amsterdam.

BSI (1979). BS 4778:1979.

BSI (1987). BS 5750:1987.

Buckle, J. K. (1982). *Software Configuration Management*. Macmillan, Basingstoke.

Bustard, D.W. and Harmer, T. (1986). PEEP: an experiment in software animation. *Software Engineering 86*, (eds D. Barnes and P.J. Brown), Peter Peregrinus, London, pp.2–18.

Buxton, J. (1980). *'Stoneman' DoD requirements for Ada programming support environment*. DoD.

Cohen, B. (1982). Justification of formal methods for system specification. *Software and Microsystems* 1, 119–27.

Coleman, M.J. and Pratt, S.J. (1986). *Software Engineering for Students*, Chartwell-Bratt, Bromley.

Coleman, M.J. and Pratt, S.J. (1988). Maintainable software by design. *2nd IEE/BCS Conference on Software Engineering*, Liverpool (July).

Denvir, B.T. (1980). The place of rigorous methods in software development. Standard Telecommunications Laboratories, internal document.

Docker, T.W.G. and Ince, D. (1986). Executable data flow diagrams. *Software Engineering 86* (eds D. Barnes and P.J. Brown), Peter Peregrinus, London, pp.352–70.

DTI (1985). *Software Tools for Application to Large Real-Time Systems: the STARTS Guide*. DTI, London.

EEA (1983). *Establishing a Quality Assurance Function for Software*. Electronic Engineering Association, London.

ESPRIT (1986). *A Basis for a Portable Common Tool Environment (PCTE), Functional Specifications*, 4th edn. UK.

Evans, M.W. and Marciniak, J. (1987). *Software Quality Assurance and Management*. Wiley, New York.

Finklestein, A. and Potts, C. (1986). Structured common sense: the elicitization and formalization of system requirements. *Software Engineering 86* (eds D. Barnes and P.J. Brown), Peter Peregrinus, London, pp.236–50.

Flynn, D.J., Layzell, P.J. and Loucopoulos, P. (1986). Assisting the analyst – the aims and approaches of the analyst assist project. *Software Engineering 86* (eds D. Barnes and P.J. Brown), Peter Peregrinus, London, pp.19–26.

Frewin, G.D. and Hatton, B.J. (1986). Quality management – procedures and practices. *IEE Software Engineering Journal* 1, 29–38.

Gannon, J.D., Katz, E.E. and Basili, V.R. (1986). Metrics for ADA packages – An initial study. *Communications of the ACM* 29, 616–23.

Garvin, D. A. (1984). What Does 'Product Quality' Really Mean?. *Sloan Management Review*, Fall issue.

Gilb, T. (1976). *Software Metrics*. Chartwell-Bratt, Lund, Sweden.

Gilb, T. (1979). A comment on the definition of reliability. *ACM Software Engineering Notes* 4.

Heninger, K.L. (1980). Specifying software requirements for complex systems: new techniques and their application. *IEEE Transactions on Software Engineering* SE–6, 2–13.

Higgs, M. (1987). A clear case. *Computer Weekly*, (25 June), 34.

IEE (1985). *Guidelines for the Documentation of Software in Industrial Computer Systems*. IEE, London.

Jackson, M.I. (1983). Future developments in design methodologies. *Software Engineering Developments* (ed. P. Wallis), Infotech State of the Art Report 11(3).

Jackson, M.I., Denvir, B.T., Harwood, W.T. and Tate, A.R. (1982). An overview of software development methodologies. Standard Telecommunications Laboratories, internal document.

Jeremaes, P., Khosla, S. and Maibaum, T.S.E. (1986). A modal (action) logic for requirements specification. *Software Engineering 86* (eds D. Barnes and P.J. Brown), Peter Peregrinus, London, pp.278–94.

Jones, C.B. (1980). *Software Development: A Rigorous Approach*. Prentice Hall, Hemel Hempstead.

Kaposi, A. and Kitchenham, B. (1987). The architecture of system quality. *Software Engineering Journal* **2**, 2–8.

Kitchenham, B. (1987). Software quality modelling, measurement and prediction. *Software Engineering Journal* **2**, 105–113.

Kitchenham, B. and McDermid, J.A. (1986). Software metrics and integrated support environments. *IEE Software Engineering Journal* **1**, 58–64.

Kopetz, H. (1979). *Software Reliability*, Macmillan, Basingstoke, p.93.

Leintz, B. et al. (1976). Characteristics of application software maintenance. UCLA report AD/A-034-085 (quoted in Shooman 1983).

McCall, J.A., Richards, P.K., and Walters, G.F. (1977). *Factors in Software Quality*. Vols I, II and III, RADC reports, Rome Air Development Center, New York.

McDermid, J. and Ripken, K. (1984). *Life Cycle Support in the ADA Environment*. Cambridge University Press.

Ould, M. and Thewlis, D. (1987). Making software engineering standards usable. *Computer Bulletin*, June issue.

Parnas, D. L. and Weiss, D. M. (1985). Active design reviews: principles and practices. *Proceedings of 8th International Conference on Software Engineering*, IEEE Computer Society Press.

Pressman, R.S. (1982). *Software Engineering: A Practitioner's Approach*. McGraw-Hill, New York.

Randell, B. (1986). System design and structuring. *The Computer Journal* **29**, 300–306.

Shaw, M., Almes, G.T., Newcomer, J.M., Reid, B.K. and Wulf, A.W. (1981). A comparison of languages for software engineering. *Software – Practice and Experience* **11**, 1–52.

Shooman, M. (1983). *Software Engineering – Design, Reliability and Management*. McGraw-Hill, New York.

Sommerville, I. (1985). *Software Engineering*, 2nd edn. Addison-Wesley, Wokingham.

Sufrin, B. (1981). *Reading Formal Specifications*. Programming Research Group Monograph 24, Oxford University Press.

Thorne, T. (1987a). Computer aided code analysis part 1: static analysis. *Computing* (12 February), 30.

Thorne, T. (1987b). Computer aided code analysis part 2: dynamic analysis. *Computing* (19 February), 32–3.

Tinker, R. (1985). A practical specification and description technique. *British Telecom Journal* **3**, 60–65.

U.S. Department of Defense (1985). DOD–STD–2167.

U.S. Department of Defense (1986). DOD–STD–1838, Common Ada Programming Support Environment (APSE) Interface set (CAIS).

Index